Gary,

THIN PLACE

Deepest Blessings,

Campbell, Duncan, 1976—.
Thin Place: Glimpses Up There From Down Here — FIRST EDITION
p. cm.
ISBN 978-0692799314
1. Religion / Christian Life 2. Spiritual Growth I. Campbell, Duncan. II. Thin Place.

Published by Palette Press, New Braunfels, Texas, USA
palette-press.com

Printed in the United States of America
First Printing, 2016
1 2 3 4 5 6 7 8 9 10

THIN PLACE
GLIMPSES UP THERE
FROM DOWN HERE

DUNCAN CAMPBELL

PALETTE
PRESS

For Sherah

You make the stars
worth watching

CONTENTS

Prologue (or Chapter 0): Magic 7

1   Crippled & Coffee 17

2   A Thousand Years a Day 21

3   Wonder 29

4   Cavities 41

5   Top Gun 51

6   Kingdoms 59

7   King 65

8   Sick & Fun 75

9   Chosen 81

10   Waves 87

11   Ritual 95

12   Paul Revere 103

13   Tragically Strangers 113

14 Primitive 123

15 Messy Calculus 135

16 Apollo 13 139

17 Brothers 145

18 Desmond the Mighty 151

19 Thermal Death Point 157

20 Mark 165

21 Light & Dark 179

22 Now & Then 185

23 Mist 191

Epilogue: Swim 197

Every block of stone has a statue inside it, and it is the task of the sculptor to discover it.

-Michaelangelo

PROLOGUE (OR CHAPTER 0): MAGIC

You've got things in your life right now that you cannot explain. They don't make sense. They drive you bonkers, and that's on a good day. And I'm not necessarily talking about information that you're lacking. I'm talking about all the questions that start with "why?"

Why are my ears so big? Why do I love mountains so much? Why are my 20s so much harder than I expected? Why do my parents still treat me like that? Why can't we be friends? Why can't I communicate with my spouse better? Why do I love my kids so much it hurts? Will the laundry ever go away? When will I ever find the time to _____? Why didn't he tell me? Why didn't she believe me? Why do people look up to me? Why did my business fail? Why did I get the job? Why did I lose it? Why is so hard to make ends meet? Why wasn't she healed but he was? Why do I still miss them? When will the other shoe drop? There are literally a million others.

There is just so much that is unknown about our little individual worlds, to say nothing of the great big world in which we are all neighbors. If we back out a little ways we find ourselves at the "Why is world hunger still a thing with all our technology?" questions and the "Why did those lunatics strap explosives to their chests?" questions and the "How can people sell and trade other people" questions. And those can just suck the hope right out of anybody.

But I believe there are at least two things we never outgrow: curiosity and wonder. They may get rusty, buried, or forgotten, but they're there. These are vital because they're also the antidote to quite a bit of despair. I've noticed that curiosity and wonder go together more often than not, and they appear far too many times in our lives to be coincidence. Sometimes our curiosity leads us to discover something wonderful, and we stand in awe of it, like the anatomy of a flower or Miles Davis. It may have even changed our lives like church camp or surfing or ciabatta.

But this book had to be written because of those times in which the reverse is true: you are awed by something wonderful or painful or beautiful, etc., and *then* you get curious about it. And you start asking questions. Big questions. Because you're curious. Questions about life, about God, about relationships, about the lives we lead and our place in the world. Questions about design, purpose, and destiny. And when you start asking those types of questions, it can be dangerous. Those types of questions don't always have answers. They don't always make sense, let alone resolve. That's why each chapter in this book isn't necessarily meant to follow the previous one. I've written these vignettes to introduce a different way of considering the answers to the questions.

Vignettes not withstanding, I've still organized this book into three acts. Act One is about discovering the times and spaces in which something of great magnitude emerges. Act Two is about an awareness and searching for the insight that resides just under the surface of the discovery. Act Three is about what happens when the discovery turns inward.

Sometimes, as I hope to show you, an answer is not the answer. Sometimes the answer is something else, or someone else.

I'm not going to go all Morpheus-Red-Pill-Blue-Pill here, but perhaps one of the things that we need is for someone to invite us to consider things in an undiscovered way. I hope to do that in my own life and in the pages that follow. More accurately, I hope not necessarily to see something new, but to see what's been there all along.

Once upon a time, there were two brothers, whose father took them downtown to see a magic show. The father dropped them off, gave them money for popcorn, and left them. The boys went in, found their seats, and prepared to be amazed.

Soon the lights dimmed, and the velvet curtains parted. A glossy man in a tuxedo appeared; on his arm was a stunning woman in a sparkly leotard with feathers coming out of her rear like a peacock. The man introduced himself and his lovely assistant and then proceeded to do his first trick. The crowd ahhh-ed and applauded.

He went on. More tricks. More applause. Trick after trick. A gasp from the audience. Then another. Soon the claps became cheers. The boys were really enjoying themselves because the tricks were mesmerizing and the woman had beautiful legs. Soon it was time for the grand finale. The magician said that this had never been tried and that the squeamish should turn away. The boys were glued.

The magician wheeled out his special props, and the music started to create tension. He finished making his preparations and then asked for the hand of the lovely assistant, who got into position. Then with great showmanship, the magician performed the trick just as the music crescendoed.

The crowd went crazy at the payoff. They had never expected to see anything like that; they didn't even know such a thing was possible. The magician got a standing ovation for ten minutes, and the boys were as inspired as anyone. Perhaps they cheered loudest of all. "Did you *see* that? That was incredible!" screamed the second brother. "I want to be a magician!" returned the first.

After several minutes of soaking in the wonder and living in this beautiful moment, it was time to go. The brothers grabbed their coats and headed to the lobby, where they would watch for their father to pull up.

But their father was late. Very late. One by one, all the other patrons had gone, and the clock ticked on. Snow started to fall outside. It was getting later and later. The custodians were starting to clean up, when suddenly the door behind the boys swung open and the magician appeared in a dinner jacket and bowler. The lovely assistant was on his arm, but in normal clothes without feathers, her hair no longer appeared luscious red.

"Hello!" said the first brother, beaming.

"We really enjoyed your show," said the second, staring at the woman.

"Why, thank you. Hoping for an autograph, were you?"

"Sure!" said the first brother.

"We're waiting on our father to pick us up. He's running a bit late," said the second.

"I see," said the magician, as he took out a pen. "You say you enjoyed the show, did you?"

"Oh, yes sir. It was simply amazing. Everyone in the audience was asking 'how did he do that?' We were spellbound. It made me want to be a magician," said the first brother.

"Well, in that case—and as long as your father's not here yet—I've got a special treat for you. Interested?"

"Yes! Of course!" shrieked the first brother with delight. The second brother said nothing.

"How would you like to know the secret of the final trick?"

"Are you serious! I would *love* to know the secret!" said the first brother, bursting with joy.

So the magician and the first brother rose to leave. The second brother stayed put. "Aren't you coming?" said the first brother.

"No, you go ahead. I'll wait for father." So the magician and first brother went back into the auditorium, down the aisle, up the steps, and onto the stage. The first brother followed the magician into the wings and then backstage, where all the magic props were prepared for the next show. The first brother saw into the dressing room and noticed the tuxedo. Next to it lay a full head of luscious red hair on a mannequin and the glittery leotard with the feathers.

"Are you sure you want to know?" said the magician. "Because once I show you, you can't ever go back to not knowing."

"Yes, I'm sure. Show me."

So the magician began to explain the last trick in great detail. He showed the boy the trap door, the secret hinge, the hidden compartment, and many other props that create the illusion. The boy understood perfectly. It was all so clear, albeit cleverly disguised. How had he not spotted it the first time? He stood there for a minute looking at all the equipment without the lights and music and show. Seeing it all here, outside of the moment that made it so wonderful…well, it just seemed to be bits and pieces of stage set, pulleys, disguised hinges, and so forth. It was just…equipment. There wasn't much magical about it at all.

"Well, we best be off. I'm sure your father is here by now."

"Yes, I'm sure he is. Thank you. That was very insightful."

"And remember: You can't tell anyone."

"I won't. I promise."

Back in the lobby, the second brother was having an animated conversation with the woman about football, when the first brother and the magician emerged. The second brother couldn't help noticing that the first brother was a bit less enthusiastic than when he'd last seen him. He looked rather preoccupied. Just then, their father pulled up to the curb. The boys bundled up, said their farewells, and headed to the car.

"So sorry I'm late. How was the show?" the father said. The first brother, the one who went with the magician backstage, said, "It was okay. I enjoyed it. The beginning was better than the end."

But the second brother, the one who did not go backstage, said, "Oh, dad, it was…it was…just the most magical thing. From start to finish, I was mesmerized. I loved every minute, and I didn't want it to end."

"Could you figure out how he did any of his tricks?" said the father.

"Oh, yes," said the first brother, "he took me back and showed me exactly how he did the grand finale."

"He did? That doesn't happen very often."

"No, I suppose not. I feel quite special."

"I didn't go," said the second brother.

"Oh? Why not?" said the father.

"I didn't want it to be explained."

"No?"

"No. I wanted it to stay magical."

"But I learned the *truth*," said the first brother, with no small amount of smugness.

"No, all you learned was how he did the trick."

They drove on through the silent snow for several miles.

The first brother snickered and shook his head. "You know it's all sleight of hand and misdirection, don't you? It's not real magic."

"Of course," said the second brother, softly. "But I enjoyed it more than you did. While I was watching, I wasn't worried about Mum or the doctors or dad's job or school or anything. That's the real magic, far more true than a trap door and false hinge. How he created the illusion isn't the truth. The magic of the moment is the truth, because it created for me a moment that took me someplace else. Someplace beyond where I was. Someplace other. It will stay magical for me forever."

ACT I

DISCOVERING

There are things known and there are things unknown, and in between are the doors of perception.

—Aldous Huxley

1　CRIPPLED & COFFEE

1:43 a.m.

There he was. Jesus. Cooking two eggs, over easy. And yet, I sensed there to be…more. Whatever it was, it was big, deep, and powerful, like I was fishing off the jetty and hooked a nuclear submarine by accident. Something was pulling me like the silent tide.

FLASHBACK to 11:27 p.m.

I was sitting on a squeaky stool in a Waffle House in Arkansas, way too late. It was the kind of stool with the flecked metallic vinyl. Some of my aspiring-pastor classmates and I had to study for our Life of Christ class at Bible College, early on in our program. Instead we ended up talking and laughing for the better part of an hour. We took turns telling stories, getting to know each other, each of us illuminating just a bit more of our past. It turns out this can be a kind of Jesus study too. I told of my grandfather, of his involvement with Lee Harvey Oswald (really), of how he knew somebody everywhere, of how he and my grandmother are patriarchs in the movement to give kids a good scare. He taught me to tell stories and shoot a BB gun and balance a ceiling fan.

So there we were, the minutes ticking by, the three of us telling stories, pretending to study, laughing out loud every few minutes, and drawing the occasional frown from nearby patrons; Waffle House at 12:30 in the morning is not exactly filled with joy and bliss. At that hour cigarette smoke wraps itself around you when you walk in. Grease and glum waft through the air, while bacon and raspy voices crackle. George Jones croons somewhere behind the whir of the dishwasher. And there is coffee. Rich, black, fresh coffee. Pulling you in. Asking you to sit down. And, of course, you do. It would be rude not to.

We happened to take our seats at the counter right across from the cook preparing all the food as we carried on about old jobs, ex-girlfriends, and high school. And here lies the remarkable thing: watching the cook was—there's no other word for it—hypnotic.

It was subtle and brilliant how he worked, and I was rapt watching him flipping eggs in the air, and cooking six waffles. Hash browns. Steaks medium well. Bacon. Omelets. All at one time. Applied Chemistry, but with fire. The man was a monument at the corner of Efficiency and Poetry.

Watching this man, this marvel of fry cookery, also made me a bit sad, which threw me at first; not typically the emotion one feels while watching someone slinging hash. I kept watching him and wondering why is it we are drawn to sadness? I could see in his eyes that, as good as he was, he did not want to be there. There was no joy in him. That speaks volumes of a man and where he is, to be elite at his job yet not enjoy it. It's one thing to hate going to work because it's lousy or because it's good but you're lousy at it. But to hate going to work when you're the best? That's a whole different animal, and a cruel twist. Springsteen now howled *Better Days* over the yellowed speakers in the ceiling.

I suppose satisfaction is not really a prerequisite for a job, but all the same, I do not remember him smiling one time in the hour and a half we were there. He just did his job. Over and over. More eggs. More bacon. Toast is done. Flip the hash browns. Pour five waffles. Over and over. Just doing his job.

And I thought to myself *I wonder who this guy is? What's he like? What stories does he tell his friends at 12:30 in the morning? What makes him sad? Is he sad? Or just tired and indifferent? Why is he working so late on a weeknight? He should be at home with his family. Maybe he doesn't have a family. Maybe he does, but this is the only job he can find, and he's gifted, like the Steve Jobs of short order cooks. Maybe this is his second job. Maybe his wife is rich, and he just works so he can give his paycheck to the glass bottle on the counter with picture of the crippled kid on the front.*

On and on it went, me studying this cook instead of my notes about Jesus, analyzing every motion and expression on his face rather than those on the page in front of me. Another couple of eggs. More hash browns. A slab of ham. Three more waffles. Just doing his job.

I raised my cup of fresh black coffee to my lips and thought *Why am I so blessed that I do not have to become the best fry cook in town? What makes me so special? Why did I get all this favor?*

It was a strange feeling, seeing in technicolor how blessed I am. I was going to university. I had a truck. I had a leather jacket. I had parents who loved me and provided for me. So why was I feeling so desolate, an island on a swivel stool? I used to know a girl in college who consciously avoided those kinds of situations so that she would not feel those types of things, which in retrospect, seemed a bit like checking part of your humanity for the flight so you didn't have to lug it through the terminal.

No, I had to feel this cook. I must. I had to confront him in my mind and soul, no matter how afraid I was of what might have lurked there. I went there to study about Jesus, and that was exactly what I did, only God changed my notes from my papers to this cook. There he was. Jesus. Cooking two eggs over easy. Beckoning me deeper. Asking me why I was so blessed.

And yet, I sensed there to be more. Whatever it was, it was big, deep, and powerful, like I was fishing off the jetty and hooked a nuclear submarine by accident. I needed to jump in after it.

2 A THOUSAND YEARS A DAY

The question of the Waffle House really had less to do with being blessed and more about the story am I telling with my life? Because whatever questions arose from that night arose out of what had led me to that point: my backstory, if you will. What I did from that moment on hinged on the the question of that moment, which I'd have never gotten to were it not for my prologue. That's true for all of us. The *what is the story I am telling with my life* question is one we often must answer in retrospect. It's only by looking back can we make some sense of what we're presently doing, for good or ill. Then we can start to make choices that determine a new story.

But how do we look back? How do we see those meaningful touch points, those historical markers of our lives? What do they mean, and most importantly, where should we head in light of them?

It should not be lost on us that of all the means of communication from which God had to choose, he picked story. He could have picked term paper, lecture, theology, picture book, news report, or game. But in the end, he went with story. Stories are universal. Those other things have their place, but notice how the bible begins: with a, well, beginning, as all stories do. Later on, God chose Jesus as the divine revelation, the most perfect illustration of who God is because Jesus is God in human form. God chose to tell us about Himself with Jesus. But God chose to tell us about Jesus with a story.

But then immediately God has a problem: us, and our brains. We can't comprehend all that he is or has in mind to tell us he is. He must overcome the formidable task of helping us understand the basics yet continually discover more and more. So God must tell his story in several ways and on several levels. William Stafford's verse seems poignant here:

> So, the world happens twice—
> once what we see it as;
> second it legends itself
> deep, the way it is.[1]

God must tell us once on the surface of things, as they appear. And then again, deeper, as they really are. Once with words, and once with meaning. Once with that which is seen, and once with that which is unseen. It is where the two meet that we often get a glimpse of the glory. When I look back I see a thousand droplets of those glories, holy droplets on my windshield life. But he is telling us these things on both levels at the same time. It's just up to us to discover it.

God is not so uncreative that he must limit his Story to words on a page. Sometimes God foregoes the theology and the lists and the propositions opting instead to communicate through the piece of music, the sculpture, the painting, the play, the movie, the architecture, the design. Often, God has to take the scenic route around our brain and get to the destination of our hearts and imaginations.[2] If you've ever been so captured by something you cannot tear yourself away, be it Narnia, or

Mozart, or a fry cook downtown, you know exactly what I'm talking about.

There is some truth that cannot be communicated with a list of bullet points or a police report. To do so insults the material. Good stories move us. Great stories take us where we want to go, but not in a way we expect to get there, and leave us thinking, "That was brilliant," and "How have I missed that for so long?" all at the same time.

The tellings of stories are many and varied, but the core of a great story resonates no matter the medium. Poets try to take us to a place that transcends our moment with their words. Most of the time they fail because most poetry is slight. Capturing a place where the surface and the deep meet at all is difficult enough, let along preserving it with words. There are the artists who try to show us a glimpse of reality with a brush or pencil. Composers use a staff and notes. Again, most of the time they miss. Sometimes they approach it, but sometimes, on those rarest of occasions, they hit the bullseye and we are never the same. How many sermons have you heard in your lifetime? How many teachers? How many relationships? How many songs? How many movies? And how many do you actually remember?

Stories have been around for thousands of years as a means of conveying truth. Movies, obviously, are a much more recent invention, and a game-changing one at that, but at their core they are still stories, only with pictures. There are some movies (books) that you watch (read), and they're pretty good. But then there are some movies you watch, and they hit you in a different place. They tune you to a different frequency. You don't just watch them, you absorb them, you drink them in, you bask in them. Something uncorks inside you in such a way that you could watch them a hundred times and they would never get old. They elevate. They speak the language of the soul. And the more they approach truth, the thinner the place. They illuminate what was hidden before and give us clear insight into reality, and beyond that, into ourselves.[3]

As an example, I don't think it's too much of a stretch to point out that there is lot of the Jesus story embedded in the Harry Potter story, especially the last few chapters of the last book. On the surface, Harry willingly and bravely submits to death in order to protect his loved ones from evil. Then—get this now, because it's really incredible—he comes back to life and can therefore defeat evil once and for all. And love is the catalyst for the whole thing. Love is the undoing of The Bad Guy in the final book, who never sees it coming, and it blasts him to smithereens.

I'm pretty sure that one of the reasons Harry Potter sold a billion copies was that it had echoes of a far deeper and more profound truth within it.[4] Whether or not this was Mrs. Rowling's intent is anybody's guess; I'm simply saying that for something to connect with so many people—my goodness, an entire *generation*—there have to be deeper elements involved than wands and spells. There has to be something *beyond*.

And while we're here examining movies, we may as well kick the tires on *Star Wars* because the same argument holds; it was the Harry Potter of the previous generation. As a matter of fact, Harry Potter has more in common with Luke Skywalker than just about any other literary figure.

They were both orphans living with their uncles and aunts in a soul-crushing home. Both were socially stuck. Both have run-ins with strange people who let them in on a secret of their past. Both discover that they have access to special powers. Both discover their parents were, in fact, murdered by an evil archetype. Both have a guy friend and a girl friend who, incidentally, wind up together. Both set off to learn the ways of their powers from an old mentor, who eventually dies, consequently propelling our hero toward a final epic battle to save his loved ones, which he can only win by summoning a power greater than his own skill: self-sacrifice.

Whether it's the Force or a magic spell from a wand, in their essence they are the story of the Cross, and *that's* why those stories have such huge ("cult?") followings. Everybody believes in something. The belief is not the hard part. The ability to believe is in our blueprint. Rather, the question is, "belief in what?" Movies? Your college football team? Your favorite novelist? Your job? Something else?

In the Medieval world, the stories were told not by books or movies, but by the stain glass windows. Not everyone could read, and even if they could, bibles weren't readily available until after Gutenberg's little invention. So the story of Jesus, indeed the story of the bible, was communicated by images. If you've ever been to a cathedral in Europe, you know this to be true. You see window after window of glass and lead that is stunning, and has been stunning for generations. (It's worth noting that they are in the church, the place of ritual, and are illuminated from behind by light. It's a powerful metaphor to ponder.)

Standing there amid the Gothic architecture, staring up at those windows, you will come to know why they say a picture is worth a thousand words. And pictures, images, and ideas conveyed in color and texture capture us like few other things can. People discover thin places there because when it comes to telling a story, artists have the upper hand.

Further back, in the Ancient Near East, the artistry of Israel's tabernacle bespoke its sanctity and importance. In the last third of the book of Exodus, we meet Bezalel and

Oholiab,[5] God's designated artisans. They were men who would communicate the gravity and eminence of God's dwelling place through their creativity. They were chosen by God to build and decorate the tabernacle because they were tremendously gifted, and there's something about the creative process that connects us with God. It doesn't *connect* us in the church-y sense, but connects us to something Other, in the place where art has a voice that is beautiful and mysterious and makes us sound nuts when we try and explain it, because it is not from the country of words.

Isn't that the way we feel when we are captured by that particular song? We're driving along minding our own business and suddenly we hear it, and we are instantly transported back to the moment that gave the song so much meaning. Or we're in the museum, transfixed by the rendering of oil on canvas, unable to tear ourselves away back to real life. Or the curtain drops and instead of clapping like everyone else, all we can muster is to sit there in awed silence because we have been struck.

My mom had an artist friend while in college who said that he didn't get any older when he was painting because time stopped for him when he was creating. Most people would dismiss his sentiments as the drug-induced ramblings of a 60's-era art student at the University of Texas. And let's be honest, that's a compelling argument. But what if he weren't crazy? What if he'd stumbled onto some ripple in space time, some hidden overlap between our world down here and the next world Up There, a place where "time just got away from me" or where "we were having so much fun time just flew by?"

We already have language for the phenomenon, after all. Hasn't that ever happened to you? Does time really fly? Or did time stop because you were so absorbed, so intensely focused in what you were doing that you went to another place? We've all been doing something that started out as just fun, but some-where along the way it morphed from fun to precious to crucial, and it was feeding our soul and whispering to us, and suddenly the sun was coming up and the music quit because the battery was dead.

Maybe time stopped and flew *at the same time*. Which, of course, sounds paradoxical, but maybe that's because you auto-matically tried to use our brain to figure that sentence out, when instead we are perhaps in the territory of the soul. Our brain just *knows* that a hour here is the same as a hour in Albu-querque, which is the same as an hour in Moscow. But our soul can have a different experience of a minute; an hour can last a second (kissing) or an hour can last a day (in the E.R. waiting room while your child is in trauma surgery).

I know the physical body kept aging for that hour or two or seven, but what about the soul? Our souls are bound by time, but only as far as they're connected to our physical body. But what if there were a place where our soul connected with some-thing other than our physical body? Is this what an "out of body" experience is? Sure, death is one of these times, but…are there others?

And what if art and the creative process is the catalyst, the on-ramp to those connections? Or hearing a story that is so good and that is being told so tremendously that we are enrap-tured and transported? Like when we'd listen our granddad tell a story around the campfire. Or the first time we saw *Lés Miser-able*. Or that page-turner we got at the airport. Or that night when our kid started telling *us* stories.

And if time creeps to a crawl when we're being put through the grinder, but it zooms by when our soul is being nourished with joy in its various forms, what would happen if we were actually to be in the presence of Ultimate Joy, Ultimate

Love, Ultimate Peace? Stop thinking like a scientist for just a second, and think like an Ancient Near Eastern poet. Were we to be in such a place, Time would go so fast, we couldn't measure it anymore. It would go so fast, a thousand years would be like a day, just as Ps. 90:4 says.[6]

These little blips in reality which we have difficulty explaining are not just coincidences—there are far too many of them. They are calling points. They are a lighthouse on the shore of a vast and anonymous sea: they don't shine their light toward you constantly lest you go blind, but they shine in a comfortingly slow rhythm. These are thin places. And we must keep watching to make sure we don't miss them. Because if another human can create something to capture us so, what could have been created on the other side? What might lie Beyond waiting for us to discover it?

3 WONDER

We were already late to the concert, half an hour later than we should have been. I was downright bothered by this. I like to get to places early. Being late causes me dread. When I was twelve or so, we were late to one of my little league games, and consequently I had to sit out the first inning instead of starting for the first time in my career and playing the whole game without being substituted. Then and there, on that dugout bench, as I watched some scrub eleven-year old playing my third base, I vowed that I would never be late to anything again. But there I was in my late twenties, and we were late to the concert, and, even worse, it was not my fault.

The concert was at a giant church in Memphis, general admission seating all around. The music started the exact second we walked in the door, so technically, I guess we weren't late. But most of the seats were taken, exactly as I'd predicted when I said we should really get going. Yet somehow we managed to still get decently close to the stage, which put me in a better mood. And it was loud, so that was good. I could feel the bass in my chest cavity, which is one of the hallmarks of a good concert. That and lasers and fog.

So there I was, looking at lasers and cheering up. The music went on for about an hour. Towards the end it was a little slower and with blue lights. Then this cool speaker guy named

Louie came out to deliver a talk or sermonette or whatever you call the speech in the middle of a concert. And he was cool looking. So was the band, now that I think about it. It's comforting to know some Christians can look cool even though it's a tiny thing given his subject matter that night.

Anyway, I was expecting the typical sermon/talk: 1) funny story that seems unrelated; 2) obscure bible passage/character; 3) retelling of said passage in modern day lingo; 4) showing how that funny story really is related; 4 ½) (optional) personal contrition over a sin long ago 5) Relevant Application/What Now; 6) Big Emotional Ending and; 7) solicitation of a personal commitment (spiritual or monetary). Having given several of these talks myself, I was familiar with the setup.

Louie the Cool Speaker did absolutely none of these. Louie showed a picture of a star. Several, actually.

His topic was how God is indescribable,[7] which is a rather funny and ironic title; probably he named it that on purpose. He was smart.

He started out with a picture of our galaxy, the Milky Way, dense with stars and aglow against the blackness of space, the picture we've all seen a million times. It was very peaceful. Then he proceeded to give some stats about the Milky Way just to show how big it is, his point being that if God created something that big with his breath, then He's a Very Big God.

The Milky Way, he began, is 100,000 light years across. That means it takes light, which travels at 186,000 miles per second, 100,000 years to get from one side to another. With some simple math, he calculated that 186,000 miles per second is equivalent to 11,160,000 miles per minute, 669,600,000 miles per hour, 5.88 trillion miles per year. So traveling 5.88 trillion miles per year for 100,000 years will get you across the Milky Way. It is 5.88×10^{13} miles across. At this point, my eyes glazed over at the math.

All those numbers sounded impressive, but they were meaningless to me. I knew what about 100,000 is because that's how much a house cost I once bought. And I've heard of a baseball player receiving x amount of millions for his services, but I don't really know what that means even though I pretend I do. But then, just to give some perspective, he continued. And this is when I realized I was approaching someplace else. He said that a million seconds ago was...eleven and a half days ago. *Whoa. Cool,* I thought.

Then he asked if we thought we knew when a billion seconds ago was. I didn't. It was 32.7 years ago; September of 1975 as of the night I was hearing all this. *Wow. Really?* Yep.

How about a trillion seconds ago? By now I was thinking sometime in the 1300s.

Nope.

29,701 B.C.

My brain paused. My leg stopped twitching. The date hung in my mind, suspended in mid-comprehension. Twenty-nine thousand. Seven hundred. And one. B.C.

Then he hits us with a quadrillion (1,000,000,000,000,000) seconds ago. Which was 30,800,000 BC.

I became deathly still in a room of three thousand people. I could feel my own breath. People all around me gasped and smiled as comprehension dawned like the sun over the mountains.

The Milky Way is huge.

I was beginning to realize this fact, which we all know intuitively, but then and there, with those stats, space became tangible. And—get this now—the Milky Way is one of billions of galaxies. Billions, with a "b." And God created it, so says the bible. Fashioned it with his thought. The concept hit me like an anvil: This is One Big God.

Typing those words makes it sound so simplistic, but it was a profound moment. "In the beginning, God created the heavens and earth," the bible begins. Indeed. I had read that verse a thousand times. I had memorized it. I had said it to teens at the school where I taught when I taught Genesis to freshmen.

Until that moment, under the blue lights and the fog, I had only understood one ounce of it. Until then, having come from the Renaissance-influenced, Post-Modern West, I'd never quite gotten the scope of Genesis 1:1. The rest of Genesis 1 is so poetic that it's easy to miss the scale of the thing. It's a crescendo of Creation, too important for the rinky-dink, facts-and-figures style reporting we Enlightened are so keen on. No, this was epic, and it demanded—still demands—to be told epi-cally.

None the less, some simple math stunned me and made the bigger picture, well, big. It made the universe make sense and my conception of it click into place, if only briefly. I sat in wonder, my mind racing trying to take it all in and at the same time calculate the number of all the other things of which I'd only understood a fraction. Surely there was more.

There were, as it turned out. Over the next hour, which seemed like ten minutes, Louie the Cool Speaker went on to give stats and show images of planets, stars, nebulae, even black holes, each one more impressive, more mysterious that the last. There are planets out there twice the size of the earth's orbit around the sun (Beetleguice), planets so big that 7 quadrillion earths could fit inside (Canis Majoris). Louie the Cool Speaker said that 7 quadrillion golf balls would cover the entire state of Texas 22 inches deep.

There are nebulae that look as if the black vacuum of space has been tie-dyed (Ring Nebula), nebulae that look as though the eye of God was looking through a tear in the fabric of the universe, keeping watch over his creation (Hour Glass Nebula). Seriously, Google it. It's crazy.

There are black holes literally on the other side of the universe, 31 million light years away (Center of Whirlpool Galaxy), into which modern astronomical technology allows us to see. See into a black hole. *See into a black hole.* And what we find there is...design. Purpose. Perspective. As though God has been patiently waiting for us to invent the Hubble so we get a glimpse into another facet of creation. Which makes me wonder what the next big telescope, the Hubble 2.0, is going to find?

"The heavens declare the glory of God; the skies proclaim the work of his hands."[8] The verse literally changed meaning before my eyes as Louie the Cool Speaker scrolled it across the screen. No, not changed. It didn't change. It developed, as though the verse were a sheet of photo paper going into the developer bath, the image and meaning slowly emerging, becoming clearer than it ever had been.

When those moments happen, they are of such genuine clarity, such crisp and lucid connection. Like in *Phenomenon* where all the parts of John Travolta's brain connect in a way previously unknown to history. He could see and sense everything so much clearer, even twirl sunglasses in his hand with only his thoughts like he was using the Force. Turns out he had a tumor, but that's not the point; the point is that there are places in time where our leg stops twitching, and our eyes focus. There are places at which our mind locks onto a deeper layer of truth like two magnets clacking together through the thin sheet of paper between them. It's been called the "light-bulb" moment or the "aha moment," but it's narrower than that. It's thinner.

Sitting there that night listening to Louie the Cool Speaker was one of those places in time and space for me. I hadn't been to that church before, nor have I been there since. But in that church, at that hour, an entire paradigm of thinking shifted both its plane and trajectory.

I always knew that when I prayed God wasn't just on the other side of the roof, a giant, white-bearded old man hanging in the air listening to me and nodding and saying "mm-hmm" every few minutes. But it's so easy to picture him in this way, because it's so easy for us to talk to God as if he were our friend. That's the perspective of God we are, tragically, so often fed. God as Pal. My friend John the Professor said our modern world wants to see Jesus as our Furbie. That's more or less our paradigm, thanks in no small part to modern Christian self-help literature, fluffy books, happy preachers, sugary Christian radio, etc. Christianity as Product wants to see God as our friend because God as our friend sells like gangbusters. And there's some truth in it; Jesus said we're his friends if we do what he asks; the friend metaphor is not foreign to Jesus.[9]

But that can't be all about God, can it? There should be more, shouldn't there? More texture, if only we could see it. We can sense that there's more. We long to see it, touch it. I believe we hope for these places. I believe we long for them. I believe we need them. I believe most of what we do, conscious or subconscious, is driven by our desire for interacting with the divine, for thin places, because we are driven by a desire to connect with God, whether we know it or not.

Most of the time, we live in the *thick* places—all that is seen and sensed is the here and now. We can feel good physically or even emotionally, but to no greater end. But deep down we long for the greater end because intuitively our hearts and souls know there is more to life than this moment right now. And we often fall short, opting instead for the surface of things because we don't know there is another choice. We spend a ton of our time and energy on questions like:

"What kind of coffee do I want?"
"What new show should I check out?"
"What do I need to do at work tomorrow?"
"Do I have to go to the store today?"
"How many Likes did I get?"
"What do I need to study?"
"How am I going to get all this laundry done?"
"What do you want for dinner?"

These are questions designed to get us through the day. But what about the questions designed to get us through life? If our biggest story arc is getting to the weekend, something within us is off, and it will start to rebel.

I understand that at the end of our day we don't have a ton of energy to explore some deep existential quest. Sometimes we just want to vedge in front of Netflix. I get it. But if we do that long enough, our habits become patterns and patterns become a culture, a culture in which we were never intended to live. Then one day we realize everything seems so bleak. We can't remember the last time our soul was really nourished, because in some cultures souls aren't nourished; they're starved. Souls die every day in the cultures of consumerism, politics, living for the moment, the weekend, and work.

This is right about the time we realize something's missing. And here's where it gets tricky, because when most people realize something's missing, they try to fill it with the obvious. "I'm not satisfied with my work anymore" or "I'm not in love with my spouse anymore" or "I need a change of scenery" so they change jobs/spouses/cities. Those all might be true, but they're not the problems. They're the symptoms. Treating them as problems just makes a bigger mess. The truth is that the only way for a culture to change is for a death to occur. Perhaps a physical death, but more likely a metaphorical death: a drastic and permanent ending to some aspect of the culture. Then, and only then, can it move forward.

Then along comes some scenario, some chance encounter with beauty or courage or a kindness or insight. And we are struck by something big and meaningful, something whose vibrance contrasts the day-to-day, be it a selfless act or the Crab Nebula. Then the lesser questions give way to the "How have I missed that for so long?" and "How come I don't see that more often?" and "Why am I so tired all the time?" questions. Those are better because when we ask them we are starting to acknowledge that something is missing, we're just not sure what.

And if we're curious and persistent, then we're led to something like "Am I truly joyful here?" or "Why haven't I achieved more in life by now?" or "What is *really* going on with me?" or "Will there ever be a time when I don't have to deal with _____?" or "Who am I and Who should I be?" When these questions surface, they are far better than answers. Questions like these shape us and reveal far more than answers ever will.

And it's not just us today. Many generations of cultures long before us have grappled in this ring too. Because no matter what hunk of dirt you call home, inside all of us there is this longing, this tug towards something deeper, towards something More. Greater. Nobler. Higher. We know it's there, we can sense it. It is substantial but cloaked, as if feeling a sledge hammer through a quilt. I've felt it. So have you. If only we could wrap our fingers around it to pull it close and so know that there's more, more clarity, more meaning, more soul nourishing just beyond that quilt. Sometimes we can see it more clearly; there's a hole in the quilt, or a breeze flips a corner up.

Could this be why we long for mystery and why we as a people are so drawn to it? Stephen King understands this and has made a career out of it. And romantic movies and fantasy novels are more than just heroic quests with dragons and magic and beautiful people saying witty things under great lighting. They mask an invisible current beckoning to us from just under the surface of reality. Many times the story is not so good and leaves us dissatisfied, but every now and then the story resonates with us on some deeper level ("I LOVE that movie," or "That book made me cry…"), and we find ourselves at a thin place because we see into what could be. We watch, and long to watch, and read and reread again because maybe, just maybe that story could be our story (said every kid who has actually felt the Force, or longs for their letter from Hogwarts).

Here's where the ancient Celts come in. They were right there amid the search party for truth, only they had this beautiful and poetic way of describing those moments of fleeting clarity. They called them thin places.

The Celts believed that heaven and earth, i.e., this world and the next, were two very different and distinct places, close but separate. Indeed, two stories reality is telling: one on the surface of things, as it appears, and one deeper, as it really is. What separated them was not a door, but only a veil. In most places in time and space this veil is thick like black canvas, obstructing our view and keeping us here from seeing into there, "in the dark" to use our nomenclature.

But in some spaces and moments in this life, the veil is thin, very thin, like gauze whispering at midnight. It allows us to see a bit of what lies beyond. The thin place is that place where you get a glimpse into that world, where you can see the fuller, deeper picture of God, of reality and your place in it all at once. Not the whole enchilada. Just a fierce and beautiful and mysterious glimpse. And it changes you.

The more I read about Celts, the more I was intrigued by this concept. I started to notice more and more thin places in retrospect. That concert was a thin place for me, and I'm sure a few hundred others. So was the first time I kissed a girl, when I discovered the pain of losing a dog, saw *Phantom* on Broadway, and sat enraptured listening to Michael the Youth Minister's messages at church camp.

We all have them. They can take any shape, form or fashion. They are no respecter of contexts, lest we think thin places only happen at church. God is not so uncreative he must limit himself to words on a page or a few hours Sunday morning. He is the greatest teacher in the cosmos. He'll use anything to make himself known. But he respects us enough not to beat us over the head with Himself. There are notable exceptions, but most often He enjoys subtlety.

When asked "What do you think when you go on stage?", Lawrence Olivier said, "I think, 'this is my space, this is where I belong.'"[10] Which was true for him, but it's not just about the place. A stage is just a bunch of boards and curtains most of the time. But sometimes, in *that* moment of the play when something magical happens, when the characters and the vision of the writer and the timing of the conductor and the blocking of the director all converge, that stage space *at that time* is more than just a stage, or kiss, or concert, or funeral, or camp lesson. It becomes a portal. The question is, a portal to where?

Our lives, our stories, our movies, our relationships are filled with these unseen thin places, these portals, these glimpses into a deeper reality previously hidden and unnoticed. Kids being born is an obvious one. So are near-death experiences.

But thin places are seldom that obvious. Sometimes they are in Iowa. Like in *Field of Dreams* at the end when they're all watching the baseball game, but the brother-in-law and the mother-in-law can't see the players. And Gabby Hoffman, the daughter, starts choking on the hot dog. Kevin Costner rushes over, and the wife runs off to call 911, and Costner says "Wait." And Moonlight Graham, the young ballplayer, comes over and sees what's happening, but pauses. Then he takes a step off the field; and as he does, he morphs into old Doc Graham the Physician, and says "This child's chokin' to death." He whacks her on the back, she coughs up a hot dog, and Doc is a hero again, and he has his Big Send Off as he disappears into the magical cornfields in left-center.

But remember the brother-in-law? The one who's spent the movie trying to convince Costner to sell the farm? Before that moment, he thought Costner was delusional. Now he's all, "Do not sell this farm, Ray! Do not sell this farm." He's instantly converted by Burt Lancaster appearing out of nowhere, saving a child, then walking into corn and disappearing. But in that whole exchange, he witnessed something that was previously hidden, even though it had been there the whole time, and a whole new world opened up to him.[11] A death of his perceptions and expectations had occurred, and it was earth-shattering.

This is no run-of-the-mill paradigm shift. People have those all the time, like when you first discovered the clearance rack or taxes or gummy bears. No, at thin places, there is a sense of the divine involved, for you not only see the world in a different way, but see God in a different, truer, more accurate light as well.

I think subconsciously we all want to visit them. The trouble is, I can't force the veil to be thin. I can't make it happen, no matter how badly I'd like to go to thin places at will. No, a thin place has to be revealed, which is both comforting and scary, because we realize we really aren't the center of the universe. And insight is the reward for paying attention.[12]

4   CAVITIES

Entire careers have been made out of the drive for mystery and the search for thin places, ghost hunters and storm chasers just to name a few. Have you seen these maniacs? Why do they do it? To claim their fifteen minutes of fame? I don't think so. Ostensibly, it's for research, but I think they do it because they like the thrill. But what if the "thrill" is actually a desire to touch the beyond; to encounter something so powerful it must be of another dimension?

They may enjoy the kick of adrenaline, but I think they are really trying to find the thin places. I think they want to find them and stay there a while, and get comfortable because they're hoping for a glimpse of something that will make the world make a little more sense. The trouble is, you can't live in thin places. They're too unsettling.

Theologians, too, are certainly in this category, although you wouldn't think so at first glance. But why else would a person spend ten plus years of his or her life reading and studying concepts and theories on God (which are thought up by, ironically, humans), slaving over laptops, and stalking the journal stacks, all the while accruing debt with which they'll likely go to the grave? Because they like it? Because it's fun? Because learning Hebrew is sexy? No, it's because they are driven individuals, but driven by what? Fame? Security? Please. People don't become theologians to become famous.

No, they yearn for a glimpse, however brief, into the biggest mystery of all. Not that they want to understand everything, or even that they could or should. They just want a glimpse of the dawn in hopes that they can in some way show others to the daylight.

Sure they wade through all the term papers and thousands of pages of reading and facts and "answers" to get to the really good questions of mystery. But they long for those moments when something they learned long ago clicks with some deep experience now. That click happens in their brain, and in our brains too, in that moment we learned something precious and fascinating and poetic about God. When those moments happen, we have to grasp them and scribble them down as fast as we can because they are sublime and few.

Unfortunately for the scholars, I've noticed that we as people don't really connect with answers and facts. We need them, sure, and we use them in our campaigns for our point. Most of us want answers because we think they give us control. But really, they are just tools, a means to an end. Answers might give us control over the little stuff like math tests or why your wife does things a certain way. But when it comes to the big questions of life, we don't really like answers. What drives us is the mystery. I mean, think of your local weatherman. *That* weatherman, the one that's been at the station forty years, the one everyone knows and who always breaks into your favorite show in the last five minutes to tell you about a storm that might hit in an hour. Think of *that* guy.

Now think of Yeats, the romance poet. Who would you rather hear explain tonight's sunset: the weatherman or Yeats? Whose explanation is more "truthful?" Most people say the weatherman if truth is the goal. But how about a description of the first sunset of your honeymoon? Or the first sunset you watched with your daughter? Or the first sunset home together after the tour in Afghanistan? Yeats all the way. Because maybe there's more to truth than facts and answers. Maybe beauty owns a facet of truth, too. Maybe there's some part of the truth that's stunning and unquantifiable. The neurotic and control-freaks among us will deny this, of course, but that's fine. They have enough troubles.

It is beautiful to discover that there is much more going on than meets the eye, because a thin place is really about un-vanity. I said earlier it is that place where we realize that we are not all there is to the story, let alone the center of it, but we don't just *like* the mystery of the thin place. We long for it. Because it speaks an inaudible language that resonates with us in a way that we can't quite describe and yet somehow find comforting. We must tune our spirits to a different frequency if we are to hear it, because it doesn't broadcast. It narrowcasts.

It's the feeling of going/getting home, wherever "home" is. The feeling of camaraderie after a win. The sacredness of our rituals. The presence—not the words, but the presence—of a loved one in the midst of crisis. These things bring us comfort, even on the surface level. But what do we find when we dig beneath the surface and start asking the Why questions? Why does ritual resonate with us? What is it about a team victory? Why does it feel so comforting when we are sad to have someone just sit in silence next to us? And how come we feel more centered and balanced when we are at _____ than at any other place?

Mystery at its moment of awareness—not *explanation* because explaining it kills the magic—can be a thin place, when that click of clarity happens. But the moment of discovery is like striking a match in a cave of diamonds. It happened the first time you kissed somebody, I mean *really* kissed them, and discovered the difference between living and being alive. A million volts of electricity shot straight up your spine and into your brain and you felt like your ship had finally discovered a whole new world, which you immediately wanted to conquer.

It happened the first time I went snow skiing. I hated it the first time I tried it. It was awful and full of bruises. I couldn't understand for the life of my why this dumb sport was so popular. It was so awkward. I couldn't make my ankles do what they needed to do to ski upright. So I wasn't upright. A lot. But then, about the third time I went skiing I got the hang of it. I gained some confidence once I learned how to stop. I ventured out from the green slopes to a more-moderate blue slope. And went fast. Very fast. Crouched like I was in the Olympics. *Blazed* down the mountain. Shooshed to a stop in front some girls by the lodge. I said "Hey." They said "hey" back. And then I understood why skiing is a multi-billion dollar industry.

It happens the first time one has sex, which I hear is popular. It's no coincidence that it and everything leading up to it is perhaps the biggest mystery of all on this earth. Yes, it feels good, and that's why many people are attracted to sex. But again, that's the surface and it's not nearly all, or all it's supposed to be. There is something bigger and more mystical to it than simply how it makes the body feel.[13] It's something—and I hesitate to use this word because it sounds so Buddha-y, but here goes—*transcendent*. Its mystery has the power to transport us.

This is why wedding photographers get paid outrageous amounts of money; they're paid to capture the transcendent on film. Weddings are really about two people starting a much bigger journey than themselves. Sometimes that moment of starting the journey happens in the I DOs, sometimes it happens much later. For my wife and me, our reception was so picturesque it looked like a movie set. Our photographer took 700+ proofs on actual film, just to give you an idea. So we finished off the evening, had the big run-through-the-gauntlet-everyone-blow-bubbles, and drove away into the night. And when we got into the silence of the car, it was like one big sigh of relief. It was about forty miles from our reception to the Brown Palace hotel in Denver, so we got there in like fifteen minutes.

We checked in, got to the room, and shut the door, and we were both all smiles and giddy and nervous, but at the same time exhausted because after all it had been a long day. Getting married is tough work, this I learned. There is lots of standing around, shaking hands and observing rituals, and the groom trying to act as though he's paying attention to the conversations. The bride might actually pay attention. The groom doesn't. He wants to eat, then leave.

So there we were in the room, and we plopped on the bed in gowns and tuxedos, both facing the ceiling, both of us thinking the exact same thing. And my new wife said "Maybe we should just rest for a minute," so, obviously we were not both thinking the exact same thing.

I figured I had all night, so sure, why not rest. So we rested, for like five minutes.

"Rested yet?"

"Yep."

"Good, me too."

And then, even though were at the end of the day, even after all the tiredness, there was this wonderful moment when it all really began, this journey into a new world. It was slow and deliberate because I wanted to burn this journey into my memory forever. This was the payoff for all those years of patience.

Not too far away, in Genesis before the Fall, Adam and Eve find themselves at a place where all humanity has longed to be ever since but seldom ever reaches: naked and unashamed. That's when the thought hit me that this was the first time I'd gazed upon the body of a woman without guilt being involved. I cannot tell you how thrilling that was, to know that what we were doing was legal and even encouraged. I had not anticipated that little morsel, and it made everything from then on ten thousand times sweeter and more profound.

The whole experience was like entering another dimension. It *was* entering another dimension, a higher plane of reality, a place where two become one. I understood the Trinity more than I ever had before, because I understood fellowship and connection and oneness more than I ever had before, and yet somehow I knew it was just a mere sliver of the oneness enjoyed by the Trinity. I remember my wife and I trying to pray a serious prayer of gratitude, but we kept laughing through the prayer because we felt so much joy and thanks and wonder and peace. I don't think I've ever felt closer to God, before or since.

You don't have to look at something as obvious as sexual intimacy to make the point that we long for the thin places where we get a glimpse into God's mind, heart, and interaction. We start far younger than our wedding day wanting to connect with something bigger. I was a kindergarten P.E. teacher for two months in East Texas before I went to Bible College. Basically that meant I ran around with five and six year olds and wore them out so that they would behave when they got back to class.

I noticed that the boys played the same games I played when I was their age. They would dream themselves into soldiers or pilots or race car drivers or NBA players or whatever cool thing they wanted. And they always had to *do* something and do it heroically. It wasn't enough just to fly the plane or make the basket; they had to dogfight twelve enemy planes at once and make the most clutch shot of all time. They had to have a purpose, and there were severe consequences if they failed. They had a mission. And it was always insanely difficult.

Why do boys make believe these high-stakes, pressure cooker situations? You know the drill: game seven, bottom of the ninth, down by three, bases loaded, full count, here's the pitch, and…every boy on the planet knows how to end this scenario. But why?

John Eldredge says it's because boys love to come through in the clutch and to be the hero because God put it in us to do so.[14] I agree, but I think that's only half right. The other half is that boys love to come through because in that moment, that specific moment in time and space when they hit the slam, sink the shot, blow up the enemy bunker, rescue the hostages, save the girl, etc., they feel a connection to God, like something clacking into place.

That clacking, at that moment, whether they know it or not, is the most like God that they can be in their young lives. They are made of the same stuff God is made of, even if they don't fully know what or who God is. "In his image," we are created, you'll remember. In that moment of heroism, of coming through-ness, it is confirmed that they are chip off the old Block. And at the very moment you realize you have something in common with God, you arrive at a thin place, be it in a fox-hole or beside a hospital bed or in the end zone.

It's no different at the core for girls. I know there are exceptions, but most girls imagine being a princess or imagine their wedding day for the same reason, and it's got little to do with royalty and wedding planning. They are preparing for the moment when the doors at the back of the church swing open and they announce their full beauty to the world, and then later, more intimately, they announce it to the groom.

This is not some "hot-or-not" contest to which they are aspiring; this is why they were designed. Not to be beautiful, but to be beauty. Girls don't really like being called "hot." They may act like they do, but I don't think deep down they really do. I think they want to be called "beautiful," but they settle for being called "hot," because at least "hot" is something. "Hot" is what a guy wants to be called, so guys think that's obviously what a girl would want to be called. But I don't think so. Beauty resides in the core of a woman. "Hot" is a sexual term; I think every girl longs to be called beautiful, because beauty is elemental to her, what is at the center of her in-the-image-of-God-ness.

When beauty is used as a lure or a bartering chip, something is out of place, wrong, "not good." A woman's true beauty emerges as the result of her being loved. When a woman is treated well, cared for, fought for, thought of tenderly, sacrificed for, she exudes and becomes beauty.

This is why brides glow on their wedding day. It's not really about a dress or make-up or hair. That stuff is good, but it's peripheral. No, this is deeper and more profound than that. She is radiant because she can't help but radiate. The "beauty" everyone can see is the expression of the divine spark of Light within her core, a reflection of how she is opening like a flower in the love bestowed upon her.

Oh, she may look good, or "hot" if you like, or whatever the lingo is, but that is just the surface, the stuff that is just skin deep and can be compromised by culture or time or car accident. Core beauty is not bound by such constraints. It is Other. It is part of the design, part of the female soul's infrastructure. It takes time to cultivate, which is probably why not many people want to pursue it. It's easier to settle for "hot." But "hot" doesn't take you to a thin place. Only beauty will.

When I was in high school I thought sex was what people did because it felt good, and people always want to feel good. And this is true, to some extent. As an adult before my wedding night, I thought that sex was something two people in love did to express how they feel about each other in the most intimate of ways. And that's also true. And I wasn't *wrong*, per se, in my previous ways of thinking. It's just that those perspectives are not nearly the whole story.

After my wedding night, as a believer, I saw sex for what it was truly designed to be: at its very best, it is a trinity of two souls and One God. Because male and female were both made in the image of God, but they are clearly different, they most resemble God's image only when they come together as one flesh.

The thin place was this: discovering why it feels so good. Because in those most intimate of moments, we, who are two genders created by One God in his image,[15] are the closest to the embodying image of God than at any other time in our earthly existence. The two become one, consumed and consuming, such that only the other matters, not the self at all. This is where we long to be: in intimate relationship with God and with another at the same time. In other words, naked and unashamed.

A few moments after that joy-filled prayer with my wife it struck me like thunder that there are so many starving people who are eating cotton candy sex by the truckload and have eaten it so long they have no idea what seven-course sex would be like, or that it's even possible.

I lament all fifty shades of their cavities. Then I lament because if that's how I feel, a piddley human, how must God feel?

5 TOP GUN

It kind of took my by surprise when I teared up as Dusty Crophopper catapulted from the deck of the *Dwight D. Flysenhower*. I was watching *Planes* with my boys the other day, and all of sudden there was a lump in my throat. Where in the world did that come from?

I'll tell you exactly where. And every guy my age reading this can tell you the next two words I'm about to type.

Top Gun.

Not unlike most ten year olds in 1986, I was absolutely captivated by that film. Those airplanes and their missiles and rocketing speeds. Those shiny helmets with cool names. The lingo. The patches. The Ray-bans. The kissy stuff, not so much, but I was ten.

But to this day, my favorite sequence in the whole film is the title sequence. The planes are being taxied around the deck of that aircraft carrier in the early morning mist, shrouded in steam and anticipation, creeping like mechanical dinosaurs with ordinance. Dozens of flight deck crew with different colored uniforms move deliberately, hooking things up, checking surfaces, giving hand signals. It is a system, a well oiled machine, efficiency incarnate. And the music is slow but pregnant.

Then the blast shields creep up and lock into place. The engines pitch to a roar, an orange cone of fire behind the plane gleaming against the grey blue carrier. The pilot salutes. The cat officer gives the go sign, and that F-14 goes from 0-160 mph in two seconds, leaving the deck in a blur behind the vapor trails from the wings, just as Kenny Loggins blasts that iconic guitar riff.

Heaven, in other words.

Since that moment, I've wanted to fly a plane. My wife tried to get me flying lessons for my birthday one year, but the transmission of the car decided to stop playing nice, so that was that. To this day I sneak peaks into the cockpit of commercial flights as I'm leaving planes. Goodness, I *still* quote that movie. Come on, say it with me: *I feel the need...the need...for speed.*

I used to draw those aircraft, the dog fights, the MiG-28s, even though that's a fictional airplane. I used to draw them in church when I was a kid because I was bored at worship service, so I'd draw cartoons and tanks and military jets blowing up bad guys. I can't recall a specific instance, but I'm pretty sure at some point I wondered why church couldn't be as interesting and dangerous and loud as the flight deck of an aircraft carrier. Sometimes I still wonder that.

It wasn't just a passing fad or an interesting curio. I am captivated by that sequence, even now. In high school it wasn't much better, although by then I had grown a mild appreciation for the ritual, the words, the songs. It does feel good to go to church and *do* something. There's something sacred about it, for sure. But the church we went to while I was in high school didn't have much of a youth group, so Big Church was pretty much the extent of my church experience.

They were fine people, and I wasn't a troublemaker kind of kid, but I saw those people for only a couple of hours per week, and we just never connected. In retrospect, most of the ritual was lost on me because it was too steep of an investment for a 1.5 hour/week relationship. I participated and thought about it and listened while I was there, but it didn't really carry over to the rest of my life. As a kid, it was even more so. Jets in flight were way cooler.

So you can imagine my awkwardness when I got invited to a church youth group retreat by a buddy of mine my senior year. We were in English class, and he leaned over and said, "Hey man you oughta come to this thing." *Why not?* I thought.

It was unlike anything I'd ever experienced in church world. I didn't convert on the spot, but it changed the entire direction of my life. Other than the occasional Sunday school class, it was the first time I'd ever done anything spiritually-minded that was intentionally designed for my age. It was my first experience with a youth group retreat, and it was certainly paradigm-shifting. It was imaginative, interactive, hands-on, participatory, and well-thought out.

That was nearly twenty-five years ago, and I remember it like it was yesterday. One of the things that impacted me the most was the singing. This was a youth group from a fellowship that sang their worship songs a cappella, no musical instruments at all. Forty teenagers and a handful of adults all singing without guitars, pianos, or drums. And here's the thing: it was tremendous.

I'd never heard anything like it. I didn't know people could do that. And they were just regular teenagers; they weren't a choir or anything. It was so real, and captivatingly beautiful. I grew up with an organ in the balcony, which has its fine points, but that handful of teenagers blasted the organ to a million pieces.

It stirred me, and caused me to consider the waves in whole new waters. And the adults actually wanted to be with teens, gave up their weekend to be there. There was loud music playing during the rec time, and ping pong, and I talked to girls, and played catch with my buddy. I fit right in, and I loved it.

Over the course of the weekend, Michael the youth minister delivered four of the most powerful messages I'd ever heard. He actually opened a bible and with no (written) notes, proceeded to blow minds, mine foremost among them. What's funny is, today, I couldn't tell you what those messages were, which is okay. I don't have to remember what they were to remember they were powerful in that moment, on that weekend.

I believe God spoke what he spoke and did what he did in my life that weekend custom-tailored to that season of my life. It was like my soul had been locked into the catapult on the flight deck of an enormous ship I had just learned existed. The cat officer crouched and touched the deck, and I went from zero to Jesus in a weekend, and it was definitely unlike any church experience I'd had so far.

But the thing I remember most about that retreat, the thing that made it so compelling, was the Saturday night worship. That I do remember. The singing was angelic, and the message was spot-on, but the invitation (or "altar call" in some parlance), was to walk to the front of the room where a six-foot cross had been erected. At the foot of the cross were these tiny, four-inch wooden crosses we were supposed to pick up. The message had been about taking up one's cross, as Jesus taught in Luke 9:23, to willingly follow the trail of Jesus though it would almost certainly lead to discomfort, rejection, and a host of other unpleasantries.

I thought about some things that were never even on my radar before, and came to some pretty heavy conclusions in the process. I left my spot on the floor, stood up, walked to the front, and prayed the most real prayer I had prayed in my life up to that point. And as a show of it, I picked up a little cross and held it in my hands. It was so light, so tiny, like my faith felt at that moment. I wasn't ready to steer the ship, but I was sure ready to fly. When I got back to my seat after taking up my cross, I noticed Jesus on the ceiling.

I mean, it wasn't really Jesus. I didn't have a vision or anything like that. What I mean is that on that six-foot cross was draped a long piece of purple fabric. And it more or less hung over the sides and draped down in the middle. They'd even brought a real crown of thorns and rested it onto the very top of the cross, kind of hanging to one side.

But right behind the cross, on the floor, was the only light source in the room: a huge, three-wicked candle, the kind you put on your coffee table before you have kids. And the light from that candle shining upward cast a shadow of the purple fabric, crown, and cross on the ceiling. And it was that shadow that illuminated Jesus on the cross in perfect silhouette. It was shocking. As far as I remember, it was totally unplanned.

Well…unplanned by humans, anyway. God knew exactly which shadows to cast. Sometimes it takes the shadows to reveal the illumination. Someone took a picture of it, and it's still hanging in Michael's office to this day. It was such a powerful moment. In retrospect, I think the process itself helped me make the decisions. And the space. And the mood. And the ambiance. It all contributed, although I couldn't have articulated it back then.

That atmosphere made all the difference because had their been those awful fluorescent lights and a vacuum cleaner in the background, I'm pretty sure I wouldn't have come to some different conclusions. It was a thin place then for me because I discovered Jesus in a way I didn't even know was possible up that point. I'm so grateful someone took the time to put thought into that retreat, to get it right, because it really did change the vector of my life from then on.

Fast forward twenty some years, and there I was on the couch with my boys trying to figure out where this lump in my throat came from, and a new thin place emerged; it was the first time I'd ever seen both my boys captured by something—the same thing, at the same time. And I thought instantly of that retreat and airplanes and how God can use something that captures you to lay a framework for understanding Him. They are a chip off the old block. As am I. As are you.

In whatever form the beauty takes, be it another person, a flower, a Monet, or an FA-18C Superhornet, it calls and echoes to something. So seeing my boys so captivated by Echo and Bravo zooming through the sky, as I was captivated by F-14s rocketing off the carrier deck years ago, reminded me that God is starting to reveal himself to them in his own contextual way. I have a front row seat.

The psalmist says there is nothing he wants so much as to gaze upon the beauty of the Lord.[16] And since the Lord is the originator, his fingerprint is on all the creative expressions and all their collective aesthetic, which means beauty is not just an end. It's a signpost pointing to somewhere else.

ACT II

SEARCHING

No idea is so outlandish that it should not be considered with a searching but at the same time a steady eye.

—Winston Churchill

6 KINGDOMS

I sat at the picnic table with several of my friends and one professor at the Bible Majors Retreat, an hour outside of Bible College. The idea was to encourage all of us in our chosen career paths in ministry. There were several speakers throughout the morning, about what you'd expect to hear at such retreat. My friend Justin was late getting there, and when he joined us at our table he had this odd look on his face. "You'll never believe what's on the radio," he said. Several of us couldn't decide if he was telling the truth or making up a gigantic hoax. But Justin was ex-Navy. He wouldn't make this up.

We all migrated to cars in the parking lot while the podium speakers went on and on and on, until finally they realized no one was listening. I was mortified it wasn't a hoax. That was how I spent 9/11. Although the next few days were a blur, I'm sure you'll forever remember where you were that day, too, the day our world changed forever.

I listened to the radio until I couldn't anymore, and then prayed until I couldn't anymore. Later that afternoon, I sat on a cliff writing in a journal with such anger and hatred and frustration. I didn't get it then, and to a large degree, I don't get it now. The list of things humans should not do to each other just seems to keep getting bigger.

In 2016, Paris was attacked by terrorists, and many, many were left dead as a result. Soon after, a nightclub in Orlando, Florida, was attacked. There are countless others. I wish I could say I had an answer, for the people of France, Orlando, for myself, and for the hundred other lower-profile cities which are subject to this kind of cowardice on a weekly basis. I don't even have the right questions. I certainly don't know how to feel about it other than sad.

The compassionate side of me says pray, pray, and pray, because eventually the terrorists will come around to see their victims as people. The Romans 13 side of me says unleash the SEALS on their generals and nuke the rest. The positive side of me says God will serve them their due. The theological side of me says they themselves are slaves who have no idea. The chicken side of me wants nothing to do with the Middle East, let alone visit and actually do something. The cynical side of me says give them all 50" flat screens, 20,000 channels, and a dozen credit cards, and they'll self-destruct in no time. The father side of me wants to adopt all those refugees myself and hug them. The pastoral side of me doesn't know where to begin but does know a hashtag just feels wimpy. The Spielberg side of me wants to be Oskar Schindler. The Sherlock side of me wants to solve the puzzle. The dragon slayer side of me says hand me the biggest sword and get out of my way, or better yet hand me a spoon because a sword is too good for these monsters. The Jesus in me says if you really want to destroy your enemy…make them your friend.

A few months after 9/11, a missionary from Africa named Dan was in town to raise support. He spoke in our class about the work he was doing there and the kinds of challenges he faced as a missionary. All of us aspiring ministers thought "challenges" to mission work in Africa were things like no telephones and only rice to eat for weeks on end. How ignorant we were. What he told us resembled none of these, and odd as it was, it made terrorists make a little more sense.

He talked about the native religions where he lived, witch doctors and such, which may as well have been from planet Jupiter as far as we were concerned. Not the fake, tourist-y voodoo you would expect to find in a Bourbon Street souvenir shop. He talked about the real stuff. Then he started telling this one story and things took a dark twist. I admit it captured my imagination, but (to modern western "sophisticated" American ministry students) when he started mentioning those things, he lost about half the crowd. When he mentioned village shamans and medicine men who could summon demons at will, trees where supernatural beings live, and all kinds of other wild happenings, he lost the other half.

See, in Africa, most of the native non-Christians are brought up in the religious system of animism, which basically says that all inanimate objects have a soul, including natural phenomena like rain storms. Very generally speaking, they believe that unseen supernatural forces animate the tangible world, and that given this premise, these supernatural forces can be manipulated by various means. So there are witch doctors and shamans whose job is to engage this unseen world and use it to their advantage or protection, or that of those close to them. I realize this sounds very, very hokey to us in the West, but that's because we've been taught since we were kids that science explains everything, that we are enlightened. Dan the African Missionary went on to explain that science does not, in fact, explain everything because there were some things he himself had personally witnessed that eve he had trouble believing.

Even so, he kept his presentation very Western, very sanitized. But I could tell he was holding back. The wrinkles on his face were those of a man burdened with a knowledge that few would understand let alone believe were he to explain it. After chapel I caught him in the hallway and asked him what he'd really seen, because foreign as it was to my ears, somehow I believed every word. He said something to the effect of—"I can't tell those stories here." *Why not*, I wondered, but I knew the answer. You do too.

Everyone would think he's nuts and they'd withdraw support. He'd soon be back in the States trying to preach, but everywhere he would go people would say things like "he's the one who saw tree demons in Africa. Bless his heart." Because thin places can be scary. And it's easy to fear fear. It is too mysterious. Most people settle for comfortable. There are fewer questions. It's why we as a culture are so hell-bent on explaining everything, why we think stamping out the mystery is so virtuous. *If we only had the answers, THAT would tell us something,* we think. An answer could very well tell us something. But the question is, do they tell us Fact, or Truth? The two are not necessarily the same.

Maybe it's not about answers all the time. Maybe it's about questions. As Dan the African Missionary was telling me all this, I was thinking the same thing that probably anyone would think who listened to him: "Is this for real? Is there really an unseen world in Africa going on?" And if the answer were Yes, then who's to say there's not an unseen world *here?* I had been taught all my life that we live on earth and God lives beyond the stars up in heaven. One day we'll go there, but in the meantime Satan will be in our heads constantly trying to get us to gossip and look at porn. The trouble was that was in direct conflict with Dan the African Missionary's personal experience. How do you argue with personal experience? You can't, unless he was delusional and he hallucinated it all, but I can assure you he wasn't and he didn't.

Understand, I'm not trying to sell a bill of goods here. I'm trying to make sense of the things, like today's terrorists, which don't fit in the nice, neat puzzle. So something in the paradigm of What-I've-Always-Been-Taught had to give. I was forced to conclude that maybe there is more to this world than I'd previously suspected.

But that can't be, can it? Demons and evil spirits and such running/flying around trying to get me to turn on God, fighting unseen battles all around me? Sounds too Spielberg. People claim to have seen angels, but have you noticed they never claim to see the bad ones? And yet every time someone in Scripture saw an angel, even the good ones, they were terrified and thought they were moments from death.

I found a thin place later that day over a cup of coffee while thinking about Satan. He is described in Scripture as a lion waiting to devour us. So Satan's fierce. I got that. But look at that other word. *Waiting.* He's plotting. He's a predator. An assassin. A ninja gone rogue. So I asked myself, if I were an assassin—a sniper, let's say—and the person I was trying to kill A) didn't believe I really existed and B) didn't know my position—

Why on earth would I show myself?

I got a chill when I had this thought. Because the answer is, I wouldn't. I would keep firing from heavy cover while remaining as camouflaged as possible.

7 KING

There are some passages that emerged to me that meshed very well with Dan the African Missionary's experiences.[17] In Ephesians 6:12, the apostle Paul says, "For our struggle is not against flesh and blood, but against the rulers, against the authorities, against the powers of this dark world and against the spiritual forces of evil in the heavenly realms."

Paul was operating from an Eastern Worldview, not a Western, which may not sound like a big deal, but it is, because they were a lot more attuned to the spiritual world than we are. He knew that we'd face unpleasant people, unfair situations, injustice, and hatred, but he also thought that these people and situations are merely the tools of the unseen dark forces who were pushing the pieces. There is a whole unseen world going on all around us, he argues. And there's nothing in Scripture to indicate his system has ceased just because a few thousand years have gone by.

Then I did a little research on the first few verses of Ephesians 2:1-2, in which Paul wrote:

As for you [Christians], you were dead in your transgressions and sins, in which you used to live when you followed the ways of this world and of **the ruler of the kingdom of the air, the spirit who is now at work in those who are disobedient** (emphasis mine).

According to this passage, there is a "ruler" over the kingdom of the "air" that is malevolent because he sets the table for people to be disobedient to God. I learned that the word translated "air" in this verse is not the same as the word translated "heavenly realms" in Ephesians 6:12. Paul is talking about the sky in this verse and everything in it. It was (is) quite discomforting to me to think that there might be an evil force pushing hurricanes and tornadoes for purposes of havoc and destruction so that people ask "Where was God?" and consequently give up on him. Yet that's exactly what Paul asserts.

The implications of this are terrifying. Katrina? Tornado Alley? What, exactly, is going on in those phenomena? Just weather patterns? Just jet streams? Just warm air masses hitting cold air masses which in turn causes turbulent instability? That's the scientific, enlightened perspective. Correct, perhaps, but not complete. But what *is* the complete picture? Is there something more? Something...malicious? Something with a morally wicked aspect? I don't know, and I'm not sure I can know. But I do know there is definitely more going on here than at first glance.

It does make some sense out of the passage in Matthew 8 where Jesus calms the storm by rebuking it. The disciples were terrified and thought they were going to die; meanwhile Jesus is asleep. They wake him up, and he gently pokes fun at their lack of faith. Then he steps to the bow of the boat and commands the storm to be still. For years, I've understood this story as an explanation of Jesus' power over the weather. But what if indeed there was something evil behind that storm, pushing it, who could no longer stand in the presence of the Son of God?

This led me to a cryptic passage in Daniel 10:1-3, set in Babylon ca. 600 B.C. when God's people Israel were being carted into exile and out of their homeland:

In the third year of Cyrus king of Persia, a revelation was given to Daniel (who was called Belteshazzar). Its message was true and it concerned a great war. The understanding of the message came to him in a vision. At that time I, Daniel, mourned for three weeks. I ate no choice food; no meat or wine touched my lips; and I used no lotions at all until the three weeks were over.

So Daniel has a vision of a king and a war, an event not uncommon in those days. From about 900 BC to the time of Christ, the Ancient Near East was ruled by Assyria, Babylon, Persia, Greece, and Rome, respectively. All of them were major military forces. Countless battles were fought, helmed by not a few kings. Still, for some reason this particular vision really struck Daniel. It bothers him. He laments this revelation so much that he deprives himself of fine foods for three weeks. But then Daniel receives a visitor (verses 4-10), and things take a turn for the bizarre.

On the twenty-fourth day of the first month, as I was standing on the bank of the great river, the Tigris, I looked up and there before me was a man dressed in linen, with a belt of the finest gold around his waist. His body was like chrysolite [yellowish-green or brownish gemstone], his face like lightning, his eyes like flaming torches, his arms and legs like the gleam of burnished bronze, and his voice like the sound of a multitude. I, Daniel, was the only one who saw the vision; the men with me did not see it, but such terror overwhelmed them that they fled and hid themselves. So I was left alone, gazing at this great vision; I had no strength left, my face turned deathly pale and I was helpless. Then I heard him speaking, and as I listened to him, I fell into a deep sleep, my face to the ground. A hand touched me and set me trembling on my hands and knees.

He said, "Daniel, you who are highly esteemed, consider carefully the words I am about to speak to you, and stand up, for I have now been sent to you." And when he said this to me, I stood up trembling. Then he continued, "Do not be afraid, Daniel. **Since the first day that you set your mind to gain understanding and to humble yourself before your God, your words were heard, and I have come in response to them.** (emphasis mine)

Daniel is terrified. I don't think there's any way in the world this figure he saw could be reasonably understood as a human being. I think Daniel just called him a man because that's the only paradigm of bipeds he had in his brain. Daniel's companions couldn't see everything Daniel so painstakingly described; yet they clearly felt something because they bolted in fear. They left Daniel on his own to deal with whatever this being was, which he did by promptly putting his face to the ground in hopes that his show of reverence will keep him from being slaughtered on the spot. He nearly leapt out of his skin when the being touched him. This from the guy who survived in a den of lions all night long. I think this being he encountered is an angel from God, because in verse 10-13a:

And behold, a hand touched me and set me trembling on my hands and knees. And he said to me, "O Daniel, man greatly loved, understand the words that I speak to you, and stand upright, for now I have been sent to you." And when he had spoken this word to me, I stood up trembling. Then he said to me, "Fear not, Daniel, for from the first day that you set your heart to understand and humbled yourself before your God, your words have been heard, and I have come because of your words. The prince of the kingdom of Persia withstood me twenty-one days, but Michael, one of the chief princes, came to help me, for I was left there with the kings of Persia,

An angel's primary job was to be a messenger; that's what the word *angel* means. So during the time Daniel was praying, presumably when he was in mourning over his vision in 10:2, God heard him and sent this angel to answer Daniel. Here, too, are some pretty incredible implications: 1) God hears the prayers of the humble. 2) He sometimes sends angels to answer those prayers, who 3) may or may not be seen by humans. 4) Angels are very terrifying creatures, not the halo-and-harp, white-robe-and-winged cloud-floaters as the good folks at Hallmark would have us believe. They are supernatural Navy SEALS, and apparently they can be quite friendly. But there is a lurking question. If Daniel prayed for three weeks, why did it take so long for the angel to get to him? Why did it take so long for God to answer his prayer? The story unfolds as the angel continues in v. 13b:

> ...but the prince of the Persian kingdom resisted me twenty-one days. Then Michael, one of the chief princes, came to help me, because I was detained there with the kings of Persia.

Who was this Prince of Persia character? It seems that this angel, sent from God, tried to come to Daniel immediately, but the Prince of Persia, whoever that is, held him up. Given Daniel's description of the angel is his vision, I don't see how a human could contain such a being for three minutes, let alone three weeks. So the Prince of Persia must have been an equally strong dark angel who was working against the plans of God. And he must have been pretty tough if this angel in Daniel's presence couldn't get past him. In fact, this angel has to call in reinforcements in the way of Michael, the archangel. "Arch" means head or leader, so Michael is like a colonel in the army of angels.

In order to get to Daniel when God dispatched him, the angel had to pass through Persia, an earthly kingdom. But there is a bad angel and his army, angels of ill-intent and malicious purpose, whose jurisdiction was the kingdom of the air above Persia, and this "Prince" of Persia did not allow God's angel armies to pass. And they tangled. What a scene that must have been, were it able to be seen.

So to ask the question "How does God answer our prayers?" usually produces these three answers: Sometimes when we pray, God says Yes. Sometimes he says No. Sometimes he says Wait. That's usually where the options end. But when I read this Daniel passage in light of Paul's passages in Ephesians, a fourth option emerges: Sometimes God says Yes, but the answer is delayed by evil, unseen spiritual forces waging war on the forces of good.[18] And if there were an evil angel over the earthly kingdom of Persia, does that mean there are evil angels over other earthly kingdoms? This brings us Daniel 10:20:

So [the angel] said, "Do you know why I have come to you? Soon I will return to fight against the prince of Persia, and when I go, the **prince of Greece** will come;" (emphasis mine)

Perhaps the "great war" in 10:1 of which Daniel gets a vision has nothing to do with humans doing battle over tiny things like land and borders at all. Maybe Daniel had been given a vision of the otherwise unseen "spiritual forces of evil in the heavenly realms," or the "rulers over the kingdoms of the air," to borrow Paul's nomenclature, and this is why he is in such deep lament for three weeks. Perhaps he saw first-hand that there are other kingdoms and other evil angels keeping watch over them, and the thought caused his mind and soul much misery.

As I mentioned, nothing in Scripture indicates that this system has yet ceased. One day, when Jesus returns, yes, but that day clearly hasn't happened yet. Think about these implications for a second. What earthly kingdoms are around today? Who's ruling? Al Qaeda? ISIS? Who's *really* ruling?

In a morally sober moment, I had to admit that there very well may be a prince of the air over the good 'ole USA, laughing every time someone scoffs at the idea of evil spirits and demons, because he knows that the silent, invisible predators are the most lethal: an assassin firing from heavy cover.

Remember when Jesus was being tempted in Matthew 4? Satan comes to him and tempts him with food because Jesus was fasting and then tempts him with vanity by saying "If you are the Son of God..." But the last temptation is quite different and was somewhat cryptic to me for the longest time before I read Daniel 10. Matthew says that Satan took Jesus to a very high mountain and showed him all the kingdoms of the earth. Now in an otherwise historically accurate account of Jesus' life, how could he go to a place where he could see all the kingdoms of earth at the same time? Mt. Everest is in Nepal, not Jerusalem.

The answer hinges on what Satan meant by "kingdoms." I think Satan was referring to those places over which the various "Princes," kept watch, as described in Daniel.[19] The text implies that there's a whole flock of them. Satan points out his top brass who are ruling the skies with wicked power, an evil hierarchy, unseen by humanity. He dangles them in front of Jesus like a carrot on a stick. "Just bow down to me," he cajoles, "and you can have control over them all." It's the same line he used in the garden. Satan's kingdom, and therefore his marketing, is all about the biggest, the flashiest, what feels the best.

Then as now, Satan deals in social Darwinism, where the most beautiful are the most "successful." Then as now, Satan is not just about *remote control;* he is about *on demand.* Get whatever you want right now. Satan endeavors to dethrone God in favor of the self, but first he'll beat you with a tire iron or cancer so that he can ask, "where was God during *that?*", and leave you to pull yourself up by your own bootstraps. Then as now, Satan's kingdom is one of sensory overload, for that is when the Spirit is drowned out. Satan's kingdom is about more, more, more. His kingdom knows no restraint, nor self-denial, nor introspection. Psalm 46:10 says "Be still and know that I am God," literally *cease striving and know...* because God knows the value and virtue of silence and calm. The last thing in the world Satan wants is for you to think about what you're doing. He wants you to shoot first and ask questions later.

Jesus, of course, will have none of it, for he knows that the true power of his kingdom lies in submission to the Father, not battling against him in defense of the sovereign self. Jesus knows of an upside-down kingdom where kings are born in stables, where true strength means turning the other cheek, and where losing one's life is the only path to saving it. Jesus' kingdom is one that gives dignity to those of compromised purity, rest for the weary, and bread to the hungry. Jesus knows of a kingdom where loud children are welcomed, not eschewed, and where in order to get, one need only ask, not conquer. In Jesus' kingdom, he publicly humiliated death by beating it at the game of dying, robbing the scythe of any power it thought it wielded.

> And being found in human form, he humbled himself by becoming obedient to the point of death, even death on a cross. **Therefore** God has highly exalted him and bestowed on him the name that is above every name, so that at the name of Jesus every knee should bow, **in heaven and on earth and under the earth**... Philippians 2:8-10 (emphasis mine).

Because of the redemptive work of Jesus on the cross, God has elevated his name above that of any other, as a king's should be. Notice whose knees will do the bowing because of Jesus' selfless act of ultimate sacrifice—everyone's, including those *under the earth*. The ancients didn't know geology as we know it; Paul was referring to the portion of the realm beyond our own where the darkness lies. The implication? Unseen evil spiritual forces cannot stand against the name of Jesus.

There is much rich theology here, but I bring this up as a practical matter: it's the name. The actual five letters, "Jesus." If you find yourself now worried about the minions of evil lurking the skies, don't worry. If you've ever felt an eerie presence, a dark vibe, or an unnatural tingling, there's no need for angst. More directly, if you suddenly feel like you are in the cross hairs of an aggressive spiritual attack, or if you find yourself in sub-Saharan Africa, certain parts the Far East, or the Caribbean, the solution is simple. Say the name "Jesus" out loud. Not some fancy prayer. Not some pretentious "I CAST YOU OUT IN THE NAME OF...," like some show on channel 496 at one in the morning. Just a simple utterance, one name, out loud. There's no need to be timid. Be bold.

It will bring you comfort, but it's not just a name of comfort to us. That's not nearly all the name will do. It is a proactive weapon against all that would be our unseen enemy. It will do major damage when invoked as well as offer protection from the darkness. Can you see why it's so important to pray *in Jesus' name?* Jesus mentions praying or asking something in his name some nineteen times in the Gospels, and what he most often means by that is, "pray to the Father in my place," i.e., "say the things I would say, and ask for the things for which I would ask." "In Jesus name," is not just something we're supposed to tack on to the end of a prayer. It's supposed to be the *kind* of prayer we are to pray: one that Jesus would pray, were he here. But since he's not here, the best we can do is invoke his name as ambassadors to his Kingdom.

Speaking the name Jesus in your prayer, a la Philippians 2:8-10, is not just saying the name; it is wielding it like a spiritual broadsword. You may not be able to see the result, but if ever there were a subject on which you shouldn't trust your eyes, this is surely it.

You don't need to be afraid of the forces of darkness however and wherever they encroach. You need simply to say the name that saves in far more ways than one. There are many kingdoms out there. But, then as now, there is only one King, one Name. Jesus.

8 SICK & FUN

My parents divorced when I was four. I lived with my mom but got to see my dad every other weekend because both my parents lived in the same city, which was nice. Going to dad's was always a treat. It was very different from mom's. Mom's was where the school routine was, where the dinner routine, the basketball practice routine, the homework routine happened. I had a great home life with my mom and step-dad, hectic and fun and full of energy. Dad's was where the slow routine happened. The slow meals. The slow conversations. The art. The books. My mom happens to be an artist too, a professional one, in fact. But there was a darkroom at dad's. Cameras. Lighting gear. Endless gadgets. Dangerous chemicals. Tools. The stuff of boy dreams.

I remember being sick a lot as a kid, but mostly I was at my mom's house when it happened. And she did all the mom things moms do when you're sick. Chicken noodle and Sprite and cold compresses and an electric blanket. Things designed to bring comfort.

But one time I got sick at dad's house. Dad caught my vomit in his hands. Literally. He was reading me a bedtime story, and all of a sudden I could feel it gurgling north. I couldn't make it to the bathroom. Started to heave. Dad cupped his hands like a bowl, and I filled them.

Not that I ever doubted it, but his action really made me consider how much he loved me, because only someone who loves me would try and contain the mess by catching my spew. In retrospect, I didn't even spend that much time with him in those years, yet I was about to Jackson Pollack all over his carpet, which, of course, made me feel guilty. Here I am finally over at your house, Dad, and I'm so sick we can't do anything fun, and now you're holding my ralph. I'll bet you're just loving this.

Funny thing, I don't recall him complaining about my being with him, even then. Even with his hands full of bile and half-digested food, he was still happy to be there caring for me. He was happy to be there, right by my side.

It made me wonder if I will have the strength to do that one day. I was thinking of this as my wife and I were taking a walk in the park behind our house. She was seven months' pregnant with our first at the time, and we were getting some exercise. Through her whole pregnancy we'd had all manner of parenting questions looming over us. What kind of this to buy? How many of that do we need? What will we do when...? And so on, ad nauseam.

So we were walking along the path in the early fall and Sherah said, "When the boy starts to crawl, I'm going to be very particular about the floors and us taking off our shoes in the house." Sherah is a woman, after all, and a fine one. But she's—how do I put this?—prone to a much higher degree of cleanliness than I. She likes things to be clean. I like things to be clean enough. "Clean floors. That's fine with me," I said. And it was fine. A baby should have a clean floor to crawl around on. Good. Fine.

On around the bend we went. My mind was still stuck on this thought; this idea of dirt. I thought about when our son will be a tad older than infant. "When he's a toddler, though," I said, "I don't want to insulate him from dirt. He's a boy. He needs dirt." Sherah nodded. The boy needs dirt. Sure. Fine. We walked on around another bend.

I wanted him to dig around outside and put things in his mouth. "I want him to have a strong immune system," I added, trying to sound smart. And I do. Of course I do. I want him to do those things because everything he puts in his mouth probably has about a million germs on it. That sounds awful, but it's utterly vital, because it will boot up his immune system to start its catalogue of germs so that it can know which forces to deploy in order to destroy the malicious ones when they come back next time. I don't wish to retard this process by slathering him with anti-bacterial gel. All the time people are gushing that stuff on their hands, which supposedly kills all the germs. I even use it sometimes when we hit up a food truck. But has anyone stopped to consider that maybe alcohol and soap aren't the best way to keep from getting sick?

Maybe it's far better to allow your body to build itself up to *being* anti-bacterial, as it was made to do. Maybe the best way to keep from getting sick later is to get sick now. I'm not saying that you should never be clean; if you've been scooping dog poo and you're about to eat a hamburger, then by all means, wash your hands.

I'm just saying that trying to protect a kid from every possible microbial bug will A) drive you crazy and B) fail. It seems to me that a far better course would be to embrace the dirt; the boy is going to find it anyway. I will not keep my son from putting dirt in his mouth, even though it may make him sick. In fact, I expect that he will get sick, but it will also make him stronger. I know it will make him stronger.

When he's six, he may get a sniffle, but when he's sixteen, he'll be able to stave it off. To over-protect him now would be to put him at a severe disadvantage later in life, when a would-be sniffle instead turns into Jackson Pollack on the carpet.

It was then I found the thin place, right there in the park: a glimmer of understanding winking at me from the giant pecan trees. God chooses not to over-protect us from life. He knows it will make us stronger. He chooses not to rescue us from every difficulty, uncomfortableness, even pain, because in the end he has a much higher purpose, even if that means we choose to put metaphorical dirt in our mouths. Job got it right (Job, book of). David got it right (Psalm 51). Anyone in Scripture who ever dealt with pain by looking beyond the pain got it right, because pain is actually redemptive, just not immediately so.

Could this be why some of the toughest years of our lives come when we're 8-18. That period of life is when people are their absolute most vicious. "Kids can be so mean." Yes. But why? In terms of specific reasons, I only have conjectures. But I do know that those jerks in eighth grade who used to make fun of my short jeans and big ears are comparable to microbial germs. They served the purpose of preparing me for the really crummy boss I had at Subway in college.

And the time I had to suffer through a love triangle (I lost). And the time when my dad was deathly ill and eventually passed away, me holding him that time. He never vomited, but had he, I would have gladly caught it. There are other such times too, and more to come. The germs never stop, it seems.

I get that it's maddening not to know the purpose of the suffering, and it's really easy to get frustrated wondering why on earth God didn't show up and fix the—and by "the" I mean "my"—problem. But that is quite arrogant, a very I'm-the-center-of-the-universe attitude when you think about it. We sound like spiritual toddlers, eager to cry "That's not fair."

We think because we suffer a bit that God is holding out on us? Seriously? My favorite teacher of all time, John the Professor, said that only in North America is pain seen as punishment. He's absolutely right. Just because there is suffering, it doesn't automatically follow that said suffering is the consequence of bad action. Sometimes suffering just happens.

I can't think of a single person who wishes WW2 would have never happened *because* so many of our soldiers were killed at the hands of a maniac's army. Yes, it is tragic that they died, and we should pay them the highest respect because they unequivocally deserve it, but their death is better than the alternative: a madman at the helm of three continents ruling through fear and torture. Our fallen would agree; that's why they served in the first place.

Or how about now? What about the ten-year old with bone cancer? What about the family of five who is now a family of one because four were lost in an auto accident? What about the rapist who gets a six month sentence, but only serves three months because of good behavior? What about the sex-trafficked teenagers, kidnapped and made to do God-knows-what? What about the child born with a defective heart and only lives four months? What about all the darkness out there that's not personal at all? I just want these to end so badly. They cause my soul to ache.

I don't have an answer, but I take comfort in knowing justice delayed is not the same as justice denied, and that even with so much darkness evident in the world, it's still tougher to explain all the light. Unfortunately, neither of those things help those caught in the throes of evil and hurt right now. But, honestly, is an answer what they really need, or what *we* really need? A fact? A statistic? A objective truth? No, we need someone to be with us. Someone who knows. Someone who's been there.

I don't remember ever complaining at someone's suffering when I get the benefit. So maybe when the perfect storm hits my life and your life, maybe it's spiritual warfare, but then maybe it's simply your turn in the grinder. Maybe there is something being sorted out which is larger than you, the depths of which we will not know in this life. But what we can know is this: we may suffer unjustly, but we will never suffer pointlessly.[20]

Even when we do get sick, even when we fall, even when for a few brief moments we look like the wretch we try so desperately to be rid of instead the holy one God is asking us to be, even then he is right there with us, holding us, catching our vomit in his hands because we can't make it to the bathroom in time. That's what the Father does: he catches our emotional bile, our spiritual puke that is so awful the rest of our being longs to eject it, and eject it violently. He loves us that much, to want to catch it all and make it go away so that we don't have to be sick anymore. Even when the only time we spend with him is when we're sick. Even then.

I wonder what he would feel if I longed to spend time with him when I was feeling better? I wonder what would happen if I invited him to join me when I do that thing I really love to do? All sorts of things in the relationship would change, that's what.

9   CHOSEN

All this spiritual warfare talk got me thinking about UFOs; they were probably more of a big deal back when *Roswell* was on tv. There was also a show called *V* about intelligent alien life visiting us, but that show jumped the shark pretty early on. Still, there are the UFO fanatics, and that's cool, I guess. Everybody waves a flag for something.

Whether there are actually aliens out there or not is kind of a superfluous issue to me. The bigger question is why are there so many UFO die-hards who want so badly, who *need* for there to be aliens? Or Bigfoot? Or the Loch Ness Monster? Take your pick. I mean, just to give a bit of perspective, there are some who are longing to connect with something/someplace other than here and longing to connect with that otherness so desperately that they are willing to believe in it even when evidence for such beings is sparse at best and explainable by other, more rational means. Such a description sounds eerily like the current popular critique of following Jesus.

It seems to me they are standing at the veil and trying to will it to become thin, but that doesn't work. That only leads to frustration and questioning whether or not it's all worth it. The religiously disenfranchised have been doing that for centuries. Like when Napoleon told the priests that they'd better be careful how they spoke to him because he had the power to destroy the church, to which they responded that they themselves had been trying to destroy the church for centuries and had been unsuccessful so they doubted Napoleon could do any real damage.[21]

Brilliant.

Nevertheless, there are several examples of thin places in Scripture, most notably with some of the early Christians. Paul was one of them. Leading up to his introduction was this: Jesus arose, gave the great commission, ascended to heaven, sent the Holy Spirit who anointed the twelve apostles. Peter preached at Pentecost, 3,000 Jews converted to become followers of Jesus.

Then we meet a man named Saul, who made it his personal mission to terrorize and exterminate Christians. He was the bin Laden of his day, until Jesus blasts him with a light brighter than a billion-volt halogen bulb to get his attention. Then Jesus speaks to him personally, asking him why he is taking out all his rage in such a way. There he is, lying in a Thin Place on the road to Damascus blind from the light, having had his paradigm of Jesus blown to smithereens. Not all Thin Places are so blatant, I know, but this one sure was. Sometimes God is still big and loud. He has to get our attention, and most of the time we are big and loud, so he has to be bigger and louder.

Then this: Saul converts to Christianity, has his name changed to Paul, then goes to try and make disciples. Jesus tells him to leave Jerusalem because no one there will believe him if he tries to preach Jesus' message there.

Hold up. *Leave* Jerusalem? What on earth for? That's where the most likely converts are.

Because Paul going on a Jerusalem mission campaign would be like bin Laden showing up at your church Sunday morning claiming that he's converted and wants to help with vacation bible school. Think about that for a second. The pastor finishes his message and asks for anyone who has any needs to please come forward, and the invitation song starts, and nothing happens at first, but then from the back, the leader of ISIS starts down the aisle, his black linen robes billowing behind his full beard, his sandals slapping his feet like the Darth Vader of the Arab Extremist world. And then he claims Jesus.

Riiiiiiight.

Sure, it's possible I suppose (in fact, shouldn't we pray for this very thing?), but probably not many people would believe him if he did that. Ergo, Jesus tells Paul to get out of Jerusalem because Jesus knows that the messenger should not be working against the message. So Paul leaves and meets up with Peter, James, and John. Paul and another guy named Barnabas go to the non-Jewish community; Peter, James, John go to the Jews, both groups eager in their respective missions in the early spread of the Christian message.

But precisely here occurs a sizable wrinkle for the Jewish Missionary Group: Cornelius,[22] a Gentile; a seeker, to be sure; a "God-Fearer" in bible terms; but not a descendant from God's People; not a Jew. Several thin places accompany this whole process, most notably for Peter. As we pick up the story, he's up on a roof praying and has a vision of animals in which God tells him to rise, kill, and eat.

Now Peter, a good Jew, wants to be kosher, so first he declines God's offer, citing that these animals were "unclean." I'm sure God, who after all invented kosher, was a little flattered by this gesture. But then he booms out "What God has made clean do not call common," (Acts 10:15) which was God's way of declaring all foods clean. The funny thing is the next verse says that this whole process happened three more times before Peter got with the program. Thin places are like that sometimes. You spend an hour or so trying to decide if it really was a thin place, but in retrospect the answer is so clear.

Anyhow, Peter winds up at Cornelius' house where he encounters a second thin place that gives him insight into the first. Peter realizes that the Holy Spirit, God's Presence on Earth in Spirit form, has now come upon someone outside the family of God, i.e., not a Jew. Cornelius is no longer outside. No longer Unclean. Which means "family of God" must now be redefined. Just like with the animals on the roof in Peter's dream, things are changing, and not too slow.

The "Chosen People" thing really bothers a lot of people and sounds theologically snobbish, but it's related to the Cornelius episode. That term "Chosen People" has been misunderstood, particularly by Christians, for a long, long time to the detriment of Christians' relationships with Jews. Isaiah 49:6 helps us out here:

> [God] says: "It is too small a thing for you [Israel] to be my servant to restore the tribes of Jacob and bring back those of Israel I have kept. **I will also make you a light for the Gentiles, that you may bring my salvation to the ends of the earth,**" (emphasis mine).

Israel was chosen, but not to be some specially-treated family, a demographic to be favored above all others. That may have happened in the Old Testament, but that was a side-effect of a bigger plan and purpose. The real purpose Israel was chosen was to be the catalyst that ends up taking God's salvation to the whole world.

"And you are to be for me a kingdom of priests and a holy nation." Exodus 19:6

"All nations of the earth shall be blessed through you." Gen. 12:4

"All nations" is the subject of that sentence, not "you." "You" is not the point. "All nations" is the point. Sure, they had some low points along the way. And yes, it took the better part of a two millennia from Israel's inception for Jesus to emerge on the scene, but Jesus was Jewish after all, and He did die for the whole world, not just Abraham's line, according to John 3:16. When Peter has his adventure with Cornelius in Acts 10, he finds a thin place because he realized that now the rules have changed. God is on the move. What it means to be "Israel" is moving with him.

Peter may not have been able to put his finger on a specific verse, but he would have known that God was now doing in his very presence what his ancestors never were graced to see, but yet had paved every inch of the way: the Spirit of God now free for all.

So begins the spread of Christianity, which as Peter, Paul, James, John, and ever other first-century Jew would have understood it, was an extension of Judaism. From that point on Jews who convert to Jesus and Gentiles who convert to Jesus become The Church. It's not Israel 2.0, it's Israel as she was meant to be from the get go. It was the next step in the story of the intersection of faith and humanity that God was writing.

10 WAVES

There's this world-famous surfing spot in Hawaii called Pipeline that has legendary waves, waves that are sixty feet tall or more, the kind they turn into posters. Can you imagine the sound of a sixty-foot wave crashing? I love the ocean, and I would be thrown into silent awe to hear the sound of a wave that size breaking. But—and please know that I mean this in the kindest way—*there are maniacs who try to ride these waves, waves that are so big that if they fall at the wrong time, they could die.* That is frightening. They have their own lingo and style and attitude. Beach bums. They don't seem to care about anything but catching that perfect wave, and the waves are beautiful. Stunning, and flawlessly blue. Miles Davis kind of blue.

The first time I went surfing was in New Jersey. It was not Hawaii. One summer we were visiting Sherah's parents, who live on the southern tip of New Jersey, in a little vacation town called Cape May. Her dad is a preacher there for a small congregation, and at the time there was a guy in the church there named Charlie. Charlie was a drill instructor in the Coast Guard, which, I found out, has its basic training base in Cape May.

Charlie and his wife were about our age and they had a daughter and we had a son so that means you have conversations after church. So we struck up a conversation after church.

Turns out Charlie was a pretty cool guy. Turns out Charlie liked to surf. Turns out that the Coast Guard has its own private beach, no civilians. I told Charlie that I'd always wanted to surf, and he made some calls, and the next thing I know I'm being waved through a federal security checkpoint wearing board shorts.

I got out, and there was Charlie, and he led me to this storage shack where the government kept its surfboards and wet suits. I got zipped and boarded, and he was all stoked that I was there because finally he had someone from church—even though technically I was a visitor—with whom he could share this thing called surfing he absolutely loved. And Charlie was no Drago from *Rocky IV*, but he was in decent shape. This made me feel good because I'm a pretty athletic guy, but I was in my 30s, and I don't mind telling you I'd lost a step or two since the glory days. Still, I was fit. Or so I thought.

We walked to the beach, the sand hot under our feet. He said "Follow me," and we paddled out about a hundred feet from the shore, and it's all I could do to stay on the board, the main motivation for doing so was the 68° water. I was inefficiency personified, doing 75 m.p.h. in first gear. My arms felt like jello, and I hadn't even tried to catch a wave yet. Finally I got the hang of just sitting there and not falling off. By this time Charlie had already caught a wave. He carved it up. Sun glinted off his hair. Girls waved at him. He was the coolest guy I'd ever met. I fell off the board. Again. I had sand in my shorts.

He paddled back out to me and started explaining how this whole surfing thing works. You paddle out, then turn and face the shore. When you see a wave coming, and it's so many feet away, you start paddling. He was a really good teacher. He gave me confidence. I felt like I could do this. There's a delicate balance, he says. You don't want to stand up too quickly or you nose dive and eat it. But if you lean back, it's like hitting the brakes and you'll miss the wave. And he's coaching me and demonstrating, and he's really patient and not pompous at all, which he clearly could have been because he's that good and fairly handsome.

But then, something changed in his explanation. There was a moment when he went from lecturing on Surfing 101 to describing a thin place, though I wouldn't have put it in those terms at the time; I only see this now looking back. His eyes lit up as he said, "When you catch the wave just right, you'll know it. It'll start to pull you, and it's like someone hits the gas. And you feel the raw power of the ocean start to take you, and then the board actually starts to hydroplane and—," he pauses. "I believe it's the closest thing to flying."

My eyebrow raised. Hmmm. Raw power of the ocean. Flying. I was just out to have fun. Now it had taken a turn for the interesting, and I was very curious. So I paddled out and turned around, just as he had instructed me. I saw a wave coming and started paddling as hard as I could. And I missed the wave. Too late. So I paddled back out. Tried again. And missed it again. Too early this time. So I tried again. Arms like *warm* jello now.

But the sea was calling like a siren.

I waited for a wave. Here it came. It looked pretty good. "You don't want that one," he said.

"No, of course not," I said.

He said, "When there's one like *that* (he explains what *that* means), you want the one behind it."

"Oh. Okay." So I waited for the one behind it. He was right. It was better. Bigger. Here it came. I started to paddle.

Paddled like a mad man. Kicked too. Here it came. A final burst, and…

I caught it. I CAUGHT it. Perfect timing. Here I go.

Holy Crap.

Nose dive.

Five seconds later, I was gasping for air.

"You almost had that one!" said Charlie. Then this: "We've been at this a while. If you're tired, we can rest."

Silence from me, and he knows exactly what I mean.

"Cool."

So back out we went, my energy renewed. Now he was along side of me, coaching my timing. And we went through the whole thing several more times, with several more near misses. But my timing was getting better. It was only a matter of time now until I felt the gas pedal effect. I'd never been this tired and had this much fun, except for my wedding night which I mentioned earlier. The sea was still cold, but I was no longer. I was sweating. I could see the next wave. It was big. Not Pipeline big, but big for the Jersey shore. Big for me. But I was a surfer. I must catch this wave. It was coming. I started paddling. The sun glinted off my hair. Paddle. Paddle. Paddle. Paddle. Paddle. Paddle.

I caught it.

Absolutely perfectly, and I knew it immediately. It started to crest. I was on it. The thunderous crash of the wave began to sound fifty feet away heading toward me. I was still on it. I tried to stand. Only got to my knees. Then it happened. Charlie was right. Only it wasn't like someone hit the gas; it was more like they hit the afterburners. I went rocketing forward with a deep, intoxicating power. I could feel the board start to lift and hydroplane. Oh my. Really cruising now. Time slowed down, but in fast motion, like a character in a movie when the camera dollies in but zooms out at the same time. The power beneath me was so...primal. And I have harnessed it. Or has it harnessed me? I tried to turn. Ate it. Gasped up for air. Oh my.

I'm in two feet of water and foam now. Here came Charlie on the wave after me. Rode it right past me, all the way in. He looked back at me as I looked at the ocean, the board, the waves.

"I'm hooked," stumbled out of my mouth.

"I know."

Primal is about the best way I can describe it. There was a connection, however brief, between the sea and me, more real that any other nature experience I've ever had. I could feel it rumbling beneath my board, beneath my feet, beneath my soul.

And in that fraction of a moment I realized why old men still surf. I knew why there is a whole surfing sub-culture with its lingo and fashion and attitude. They are hooked too, and catching that next wave, feeling that power one more time has become more soul-sustaining than fashion and socio-cultural conventions. They have found a thin place. And they want to go back as often as they can. They don't care if they look like bums. They know something the rest of us don't. They *feel* something the rest of us haven't.

They don't just feel it, but revel in it, celebrate it. Because riding that kind of power begets passion and joy and celebration. Such a power is transcendent, holy, from God, no matter what you claim you believe in. The kind of power to which we humans aspire simply panders to our greed and provokes us to abuse each other in the name of creating advantage. But the power of the sea is power of a different sort. It is not in the same system of classification. It is other. It is beyond. But it is near. You can't control it for your own perpetuation of power. You can only ride it, and in so doing, find the deeper and richer blessing: to touch a deeper reality.

But your timing has to be spot on, and you must paddle even when you're tired, for only then you will be greatly rewarded with a propulsion far greater than your own, and one that defies description. To connect and hook into to the power of the sea is, to the tiniest degree, to hook into the power of the one *who made the sea*. The bigger the wave, the more the power, the deeper the connection, the thinner the place.

That's why Pipeline is so popular. It's not just the waves. Pipeline is not simply a perfect confluence of underwater topography and wind conditions. That's the surface, observable, "scientific" explanation. But reality is not that one-dimensional, and it insults reality to think it so. Pipeline is at once stunningly beautiful (I imagine, since I've yet to go there) and frighteningly powerful. No, Pipeline is not just a surfing spot. It is a spiritual place where humans dare to dance with God. It is a house of worship in the truest sense.

It's no coincidence that that two of God's most defining, if not observable, attributes are stunning beauty and frightening power. So perhaps the ones who try and approach that beauty and power with a surfboard are not the maniacs at all. Maybe they have a closer grasp on reality, a deeper sense of the divine than the rest of us who watch from the safety of the beach wondering why God just doesn't reveal himself and answer all our questions.

11 RITUAL

When you hear the words *Summer Camp* or *Church Camp*, what memory images immediately jump into your mind? Horseback riding. Swimming. Creeks. Free time. Canteen. Crafts. Worship. Friends. Horses. Stories. Late nights. Pranks. Capture the Flag. Camp crushes. Camp food. Camp fires. Marshmallows. Notes. Initiation. Talent shows. Powerful lessons. A week long. Hot. Hikes. Cabins. Snakes. Flashlights. Cleaning the latrine. Singing for your mail. I'm A Little Teapot. Classes. Bibles. Teaching. Refuge. Fun. Spiritual growth. Bonds. Baptism. Connection.

If you were lucky enough to go to a camp when you were in seventh grade, and it was a good experience, chances are good that you wanted to go back every year because each year you hoped for the same, if not a better experience, and because you wanted to sing the same songs and see the same people, and because you wanted to do it all over again. Each year, you didn't just want to go to camp; you wanted to go *back* to camp. You hoped all those things and people would be there to transform that week into the Camp Experience and all its ritual. For some of us, it is one of our dearest rituals.[23]

For many Christian teenagers, camp is the highlight of their spiritual year. Sure, there's church. Yes, there are youth group and retreats and devotionals and mission trips. But then there's camp. There's just something about it. I'm a minister to students. I've seen it happen countless times. Then we grow up and get jobs, and we stop going to camp. And I think our collective souls suffer for it.

When camp is done well, when the ritual is done well, I will argue that it is the single most transformative ritual in a young person's life. There might be single events that are more life-changing like going to another country or losing a friend. But in terms of *ritual,* camp has the power to transport us to someplace else, someplace other. It did for me, and I only went as a camper one year, the year I was a senior in high school. After that, I had to engage the ritual as a counselor/adult-type.

Do you remember the first time you went to camp? Or every time you went to camp? Do you grin even now as you think about it? As I mentioned, I was eighteen when I first went. There was something about it that resonated with me, and the journey of my spiritual growth began to be set in motion. At least that's how I remember it. I'm sure some of my counselors from back then would disagree and say that I was the poster child for Arrogance who couldn't get enough of himself, but I'm writing this, not them, so they can just zip it.

That summer, we pulled up in our church bus to this dry, dusty church camp in rural Oklahoma that had been built in the seventies. The softball backstop was all marred and misshapen. The wooden benches in the canteen area were worn nearly to nubs. There were exactly two air conditioners in the whole camp and neither of them was anywhere near the cabins.

Our youth group had never been to this camp before; they'd decided to switch camps the year I went. So this place was new to us all, but especially to me because it wasn't just the venue of the ritual that was new, it was the experience of the ritual. And Michael the Youth Minister from our church was actually one of the speakers, so that was cool.

We got out and started unloading our stuff, and then we all met in the mess hall an hour later. Jack the Camp Director, a huge man with a gruff voice and hands the size of ham hocks, marched right over to the table where I was sitting and started laying into my friend Scott and me about why we should not be wearing our baseball hats indoors and how we'd better show some respect or else. And Scott and I both looked at each other, and we just knew it was going to be an awful week.

An hour later when we'd all gathered in the chapel after dinner, Jack the Camp Director, started—*started*—the week of camp by giving a five-minute rant on rules and all the things we were *not* to do in the week to come. No smile, no "Welcome to Camp!" Nothing positive. At all. A hundred teenagers just sat and listened to a beat down. Scott and I looked at each other wondering how anyone in charge of anything could be this bad at P.R. At that point, it was beyond *this is going to be an awful week.* Now it was *we've made a terrible, terrible mistake.*

Then we started to sing. And it wasn't like singing back home at church. No, it…ascended. It was fresh, and alive, and haunting. That's when I knew something was different. I wasn't sold yet, but the fog had started to lift, and at least I was thinking it was worth giving it a chance.

It took a bit to start clicking, but after the first few days I kind of got into a rhythm. It became enjoyable. The ritual was still new, but becoming warm and firm, like concrete several hours after it's been poured. I made some crafts and made some friends and talked to girls and played softball. It was fun. The lessons were good and the singing was as amazing as ever.

And then came Thursday night. Michael the Youth Minister was to be the evening's speaker. Now I'd heard Michael preach and teach before, and let me tell you, the guy is inspiringly gifted. But nothing could have prepared me, or any of us for that night. If you ever went to camp, you probably have a similar story from your camp experience. We were all in the chapel and the worship was simply tremendous: loud and beautiful and contagious. We sang for what seemed like two hours. And then Michael stood up to speak. We opened our bibles. He began.

As he went on, I dialed in more and more. So did everyone. He read. He explained. He paraphrased. He illustrated. He taught. He storied. He lamented. He encouraged. He challenged. He moved. People cried. People confessed. People prayed. People cheered. People hugged. He definitely owned the room, but it wasn't about him at all. It was a defining moment of the ritual.

As he spoke everything just sort of faded away, and all I could see was him. It was hypnotic. And his words changed me; his delivery changed me; God spoke through him. I had never seen or heard that kind of thing happen, so it freaked me out a little bit, like maybe I was nuts; but as soon as I started having those kinds of thoughts, they were chased away by the next powerful thing he said. He wove together a lesson so powerful, so true, so noble that when he was done not a single person applauded; we all just sat there in stunned silence. I had lost track of time. It was one of *those* lessons. It was a thin place.

But it wasn't the lesson itself that was the thin place, it wasn't *what* he said by itself. It was all of it. The community, the worship, the hour, the place, the substance of the lesson, the prophetic delivery, the responses. The confluence of it all at the same time led us to the veil and gave us a glimpse of what lay beyond. The ritual was more than the ritual. And I felt, in very tangible ways—but at the same time intangibly—what church, what a real community of faith, must look like, because thin places always lead to revelations and epiphanies.

Right then and there, I decided that camp must be a part of my life forever. I loved the community that much. I would be back next year, and the year after that. And I did come back the next year, as a counselor. And Michael was to speak three times during the week that year, not just one. The first night he stood up to speak everyone was on the edge of their seats in anticipation of what God was going to say through him that night, having remembered and been inspired by the year before. We'd seen how God could move at camp. We'd been part of the ritual, and we were hoping for a repeat. And the ritual was good.

Ritual orients us, but sets us free. It calms us with contagious and creative energy. It grounds us, but it lifts us up. It gives us something to look forward to by giving us something to look back on. This is the sublime paradox of ritual. It takes us backward to the place to which it's leading us forward. Therein lies its power. The Passover feast is not just a memorial of the tenth plague in Egypt, but a summons to hope in a new kind of salvation, a new normal: an exodus from the slavery of sin.

What are our rituals? By definition, they are not one-time events. They are *repeatable* nuggets of access to meaning and, if you're lucky, truth. Rituals exist all over the world, throughout all eras of time. Some are religious, like the Lord's supper. Some are not, like fraternity initiation or boot camp. They bond us together by making us distinct from others because they are shared experiences that are bigger than the participants. Such as eating dinner together with your family. College football on Fall Saturdays. The Thanksgiving meal. Driving school. Birthdays. Voting. The Family Vacation. The Homecoming game. Presents on Christmas morning. That romantic restaurant you share with your spouse, your Date Place. That special thing you do with each of your children when they reach that certain age. Baseball road trips. Hot wings with the guys on Tuesdays. Camping. Daddy-daughter dates. Buying the dress, etc.

Seating arrangements in the high school cafeteria (or work?) are another huge ritual which is not about food at all but about social class and connection. There are thousands of others. Something to which so many people gravitate cannot be coincidence.

On weekends, we gather at a large building with many other people. We sit and watch and listen to a message wherein a particular worldview is espoused and from which we try to extract some meaning. Sometimes we get some interpretational help, but sometimes not. Sometimes it's boring, but sometimes it's magical and makes us appreciate the truth under the message as it inspires us. Sometimes it's aimed more at kids. Sometimes its just for grown-ups. Then we leave and share the message and our thoughts on the message with others, whether or not we liked/agreed with it. Or sometimes we keep it to ourselves because we want the experience to remain within us, untouched and pristine.

This is not the ritual of Church. This is the ritual of the theater, film *or* stage. Listen to how screenwriting/story guru Robert McKee talks about it:[24]

To the film audience, entertainment is the ritual sitting in the dark, concentrating on a screen in order to experience the story's meaning, and with that insight, the arousal of strong, at times even painful emotions, and as the meaning deepens, to be carried to the ultimate satisfaction of those emotions. We go to the movies to enter a new, fascinating world, to inhabit vicariously another human being who at first seems so unlike us and yet at is like us, to live in a fictional reality that illuminates our daily reality. **We do not wish to escape life but to find life,** to use our minds in fresh, experimental ways, to flex our emotions, to enjoy, to learn, to add depth to our days (emphasis mine).

This is precisely why I saw *Raiders of the Lost Ark* six times—*six times*—in the theater when I was a wee lad. I wanted to be Indiana Jones. I was Indiana Jones. That film kindled the fire of adventure that resides in every boy, and I was a changed person from the moment I heard the first note of John Williams' epic score. After that movie, I swung from every vine I could, added a bullwhip to my Christmas list, and went on treasure hunts for my birthdays. But is that all there is to it? Just a great story and killer music and a leather jacket? Of course there's more. There is always more.

The truth is we all have a *Raiders of the Lost Ark*; some piece of film, literature, or art that, even though it's secular, resonates with us so profoundly that we will never be the same after having experienced it. McKee again: "A fine work of art—music, dance, painting, story—has the power to silence the chatter in the mind and lift us to another place."[25] Which is why we return to it again and again. Ritually.

I have a scene like that. It's a scene in *Dead Poets Society*. *That* scene. The one where Ethan Hawke is terrified to get up in front of everyone for the in-class poetry reading assignment. He's agonized over it for a week. He'd opt for amputation if he could. So he throws in the towel and doesn't do it; perfectly happy with a zero just so he doesn't have to get up on stage. But Robin Williams won't let him off that easily.

Instead he pulls young Ethan up in front of the class and starts to coach him, like a fencing master teaching his protege. Don't think, just compose. Volume. Flow. Energy. Adjectives. Nerves. A poem is being born. Verbs. More energy. Ethan starts to find his groove. More adjectives. More energy. Powerful verbs. Finds his groove. Really flowing now. Then Robin puts his hand over Ethan's eyes to enhance the concentration and they start spinning in a circle (dancing?), and the camera tracks them, and Robin is reaching down inside this kid's soul and pulling out something profound, but really all he does is launch the plane and then Ethan's soul takes over and goes where it has been longing to go all week, probably longer.

Out of him erupts this poem of such beauty and magnitude that the walls nearly shake. It comes from another place. Then it stops because he is finished. And he comes back from that place and opens his eyes to find the class, including himself, silent and slack-jawed with awe. It is one of those moments that exemplifies precisely why you remember your favorite teacher of all time. Ethan's, and your, soul had been given a bigger map.

Sure Ethan visited a thin place, even if he didn't realize it. But the bigger point is that there was something inside him to which his soul responded. There is something in us with which our poetry moment resonates. For it takes two objects to create resonance. So what is that *other* thing? The Teacher in Ecclesiastes offers: "He has made everything beautiful in its time. Also, he has put *eternity into man's heart*, yet so that he cannot find out what God has done from the beginning to the end," (emphasis mine).[26]

What is this *eternity* in my heart? How do I explore *that*?

12 PAUL REVERE

It sounds to me as though Mr. McKee is longing for something more, something truer, higher, deeper, and turns to movies to try and take him to that place. After having read his book, story seems to be his religion, the theater, his church. He has a razor keen grasp on the human condition; his book is worth a read for that aspect alone. Ironically, in his book he could be describing Christianity *as it should be*, which I think it is pretty prophetic given that Mr. McKee is a self-proclaimed atheist. This, of course, is nonsense because everybody believes in some kind of god, particularly the kinds we can wrap our heads around.

In fact, in the last four hundred years, the church has followed the academy in that it is the *mind* that longs to be, in McKee's parlance, paid off and to find resolution (thank you, Mr. Enlightenment). So in the Church Ritual, sermons evolved into logical lists, proposition fests, clogs of syllogisms and proof-texts, the aim of which is to argue the audience into logical settlement. These are the sermons that have three points that all start with the same letter, and whose main purpose is to *explain*. It's the Information Transfer model of spiritual growth. One day at lunch I overheard a friend's critique of the previous Sunday's sermon, and what she said nearly made me choke. She thought that this preacher she'd heard was such a good speaker because, drum roll please, *he had an organized outline, he had his points, he made them, and he was done on time.*

Wait. What?

Sermons are not supposed to be balance sheets delivered by accountants. They are to be written and delivered by prophets with a good deal of artistry. In the balance sheet sermon, the anecdotal and fictitious story is simply an "illustration" of the *real* point; it's just more proof for the argument—because conversion to the Gospel, so goes the thought, is simply a matter of having all the facts and having a proper understanding. Get the facts, think about them logically, and you will obviously conclude that Jesus is the Way, Truth, and Life in whom you must now—gasp—*believe.*

And if someone disagrees, it is because they don't have the correct facts, and/or their logic is faulty, so they therefore have arrived at an erroneous conclusion, a conclusion which could be corrected with more explanation of the right facts. But if you have *all* the facts, it's not faith, is it?

Ah, but Story. Story conveys truth too, most of the time better than facts ever will. Because sometimes facts get in the way of truth. My friend George the Family Minister pointed out to me that there is huge difference between Henry Wadsworth Longfellow's poem "Paul Revere's Ride," and what actually happened that night in 1775. Full disclosure, I'm not trying to write a dissertation on the topic, so Wikipedia will have to do here.

Longfellow's poem paints the picture that the signal lantern in the Old North Church as being *for* Revere, not *from* him, as was actually the case. Revere did not receive the lantern signal, but was the one who orchestrated the events of the night. He then crossed the river not by rowing himself as in the poem, but by being rowed by three people who were waiting on him.[27] Then this:[28]

> Longfellow gave sole credit to Revere for the collective achievements of three riders (as well as the other riders whose names do not survive to history). In fact, Revere and William Dawes rode from Boston to Lexington to warn John Hancock and Samuel Adams that British soldiers were marching from Boston to Lexington to arrest Hancock and Adams and seize the weapons stores in Concord. Revere and Dawes then rode toward Concord, where the militia's arsenal was hidden. They were joined by Samuel Prescott, a doctor who happened to be in Lexington. Revere, Dawes, and Prescott were stopped by British troops in Lincoln on the road to nearby Concord. Prescott and Dawes escaped, but Revere was detained and questioned, and then escorted at gunpoint by three British officers back to Lexington. Prescott and Dawes got separated, but Revere was detained and questioned and then escorted at gunpoint by three British officers back to Lexington. Of the three riders, only Prescott arrived at Concord in time to warn the militia there.

I don't detract from Mr. Revere and his heroism; I have the greatest respect for our forefathers. My point is that with the history books' help alone, Revere would have become an event so minor it barely warrants a mention. But with the help of a master storyteller, Revere's journey became etched into the Epic American Mythos and that was a very good thing, not a bad thing, because in this case Epic Myth/Poetry teaches a much truer lesson, however "inaccurate," than the facts ever could. It's not a question of which retelling of events is more accurate. "More accurate" is not the point. The point was heroism, cleverness, and patriotism.[29] When those are your aim, Story is a far better arrow in your quiver.

See, it's not possible to report all the facts, which means you have to select which facts to report, and the manner in which you report them, which means you omit other facts. And which facts you include and which ones you omit are based on your worldview and your agenda. It's CNN vs. Fox News.

The bible, you'll remember, is not primarily a list of rules and facts, at least as we would define *facts*. It is a narrative. Even the parts that are lists of rules and facts are couched in the middle of a narrative, a journey from here to there. The so-called Historical Books are certain type of history: a slanted view with a huge bias toward God. In fact, most of the bible is an argument for YHWH-driven monotheism at a time in history when such an idea was ludicrous.

Story is a different animal. We are drawn to Story, McKee believes, because Story gives us the emotional payoff we crave. I'm sure that's true, but I'm also sure it's not *completely* true. He just errs in the other direction, i.e., in feeding the emotions rather than the mind. But God gave us brains and logic just as he gave us emotions, to say nothing of the Spirit's role.

None of these big three elements of human psyche bear God's image in us by themselves; we must engage them all if we are to glimpse God, for only then are we most like him, only then do we realize we reflect him in whose image we are made. To emphasize the feeding of the "more virtuous" element to the exclusion of the other two misses the point entirely. You cannot separate the emotions from logic from the Spirit, however adept we become at trying. The reality is they grow or die together.

You have felt the hand of God right beside you as you went through the death of a loved one while grappling with the question *why did this happen?* You've felt the tug when your physical self is telling you yes, but your Spirit and your mind is telling you no. Even the ghosts of Christmas Past, Present, and Future appeal to the Facts (events that led to Scrooge's state in life), Emotions (Tiny Tim and his gimpy leg), and Final Judgment (the gravestone for George C. Scott, the burning casket for Bill Murray). You can *appeal* to one without the other two, but they will only *grow* in concert.

You think about something. You pray about it too. But you also listen to your gut. Unless all three are there, something will be off, and you may not be able to put your finger on it. There are no Sherlocks or Dr. Houses, the hyper-logical masters of deduction, which means neither are there faith healers and people who claim to be more equaler[30] than others in terms of the Spirit.[31] There are indeed people who act on every whim and emotion without thought of consequences—they are called sociopaths.[32]

In any case, you can't *just* feel. You interpret every feeling with thought and reflection, even if that thought is 'I don't know what this means.' And you can't *just* think without there being a memory or new experience attached to it, both of which cue emotions, even if the emotion is boredom or apathy. There is a *physical* dimension too, a need to touch, feel, and hear, and all of these are primarily ways in which truth is conveyed, not the truth itself.

The Lord knows this, which is why he gave Israel the sacrificial system. It was a means of connecting the meaning with the act. There was meaning *in* the act. It was more than facts; it was the experience. Every time a lamb's throat was slit and life spilled out, it was designed to cause a moment of pause and reflection on God and self, first in the priest, then in the people present.

Centuries later, the same holds true for baptism. One goes through the ritual of metaphorically dying in the water in order to be resurrected to new life, and with it, the indwelling Holy Spirit.[33] That's how the first-century Christians saw it, a carry-over from the Judaic ritual cleansing. It is designed to give the convert an act to go through so that he may connect with God, and *know* he connects with God. But seeing the act of baptism as the main thrust misses the point entirely.

There are those who make baptism the god. They would have emotion-filled dunking (at summer camp, perhaps?) matter far more than the day-to-day walk that begins moments after. In this type of conversion, I believe the spiritual aspect has been ignored. Have a nice, logically-inductive bible study that concludes with baptism as the obvious final step, or have an emotionally moving worship service during which the person is moved to be baptized, and presto, a Christian is (re)born.

But the proof that something is amiss in this common scenario is what happens a few months or years later: upon understanding some deeper truths about the faith, the convert decides she didn't *know enough* before, so she needs be re-baptized. (Note the emphasis on the knowing, rather than the believing.) The intellectual and emotional haven't been ignored here; they've been put on a pedestal.

On the other hand, loads of people say the Sinner's Prayer, invite Jesus into their heart, say "amen," and then have absolutely no idea whether or not it worked. So they try to look up Sinner's Prayer in scripture to get some guidance only to find that there is no Sinner's Prayer in the bible. The one praying is left on his own to figure out whether or not the conversion took. And if he happens to cuss or look at porn in the next few days, then he'll end up doubting whether his conversion ever happened.

With no physical marker, no intellectual guidance from scripture, he'll be hard-pressed to find some certainty, until the next altar call in which he feels a different emotion. *So this must be what it feels like to really feel brokenness,* he thinks and concludes that his previous conversion wasn't a real conversion.

But it shouldn't be this hard, should it? God would have left room for some faith/doubt, but surely he made it so that we could at least know what to do. For something as important faith, surely he wouldn't have left it all to, well, faith?

Because in either case—animal sacrifice, baptism, sinner's prayer—God is still God no matter what. God would still be God if no one ever sacrificed a single animal in ancient Israel, and he would still be God if no one were ever baptized. We often think in terms of our giving our sacrifices to God, but the truer angle is that he gave these gifts *to us,* for us to have some physical, tangible ways to drive down a stake and say, "*That* was the day I became a person of faith, *that* was the day the Holy Spirit started to live inside me." But now, as then, what happens when the act of baptism, or any ritual, is done without the spiritual, emotional, and intellectual? You just get wet. You just say the words of the prayers, not actually pray the prayers themselves. You start to use phrases like "spiritual rut" or "going through the motions."

But what if the thing inside us that is craving a payoff through the ritual is not our mind or our emotions, but rather our soul and our emotions and our mind at the same time? *He had an organized outline?* How about, *Was I challenged and inspired?* as a measure of sermon quality? How about, *Did these words speak truth to me where I am and usher me into God's presence?*

I'm thankful to John Maxwell for this illuminating morsel:[34]

President Abraham Lincoln, an incredible communicator, was known during the Civil War to attend a church not far from the White House on Wednesday nights. The preacher, Dr. Gurley, allowed the president to sit in the pastor's study with the door open to the chancel so he could listen to the sermon without having to interact with the crowd. One Wednesday evening as Abe Lincoln and a companion walked back to the White House after the sermon, the president's companion asked, "What did you think of tonight's sermon?" "Well," Lincoln responded, "it was brilliantly conceived, biblical, relevant, and well-presented."

"So, it was a great sermon?"

"No," Lincoln replied. "It failed. It failed because Dr. Gurley did not ask us to do something great.

Asking greatness was the preacher's responsibility, as Abe saw it. So how about *Was greatness asked of me today?* as a measure of a sermon? Panoplies of preachers offer altar calls and invitations to know Jesus, but again those aren't the *how*, those are the *what*. What if the *how* is a sermon full of poetry and flight and wonder, not propositions and emotional manipulation? You can see why there are so few exceptional preachers—doing the job well is exhausting and difficult.

Jesus did all of these when he spoke; all this time saying, in essence, to the so-called Enlightened establishment, "No, dude. The parable's not the illustration for the sermon. The parable *is* the sermon." And what if he's saying "You might figure some of this out, but you'll never figure out all of it, so learn to embrace the beauty of the mystery. Learn to live in the tension of the unresolved."[35] Or what if he's saying, "There are weightier and lighter matters in what God says,[36] and you're gonna have to use your brain to figure it out. The life of faith is not all praise and prayer. At some point, you gotta leave church and think up a game plan about how you're gonna live, and then actually go do it."

13   TRAGICALLY STRANGERS

Why is it that the information-driven lectures/sermons leave us feeling disconnected from the ups and downs of real life? Most of us don't tangle with the ins and outs of Greek and Hebrew grammar Monday through Saturday. We want to know how to become master of our temptations instead of their mastering us. We want to know how to be a hero to our kids and wives. We want to know how to see the beauty in the mirror, not the so-called "faults," how to be a better boss, and why our app choices matter. That's where we live.

Indeed, feelings, soul, and mind need each other in order to live.[37] When we try to grow them independently of each other, the result is the exact opposite of what we intend, and that's best-case scenario. In a worst-case scenario we have a break from reality. Chesterton said, "The madman is not the man who has lost his reason. The madman is the man who has lost everything except his reason."[38]

On the other hand, the emotio-worships of mood and atmosphere may sparkle and shine bright but leave us without depth and insight. Repeating the same chorus two dozen times leaves us longing for the poetic hymnody of Isaac Watts ("When I Survey the Wondrous Cross," anyone?). No, the heart, mind, and Spirit all work in concert but with different instruments, playing in harmony. The question is whether and to what extent we realize this arrangement, and get on with the dancing.

So how does one feed the soul/emotions/mind at the same time? By telling stories, and telling them well. This engages the ritual as a means, not an end, just as Jesus did. You have to be in a certain context/auditorium/podium to get people to listen to a lecture. But people will listen to a story any time. There's power in the delivery, not just the subject matter. Jesus knew that stories which deserve to be told deserve to be told well. There can and should be just as much illumination in the telling as in the essence.

Or take the ritual of bible reading. Some do it at a specific time of day. Some do it when they think about it. Some don't do it at all. Some do it after they run. Some do it in the morning, some in the evening, some on weekends. Some on planes, some at beaches, some at school, some at home, some standing, some on their knees. Some need a certain bible. Some need a pen and pad.

Being in a bible reading routine is certainly good. Just so long as we remember that the routine, the ritual, is never the point. The routine is a tool to get us to the real point. Jesus said to the professional bible studiers of his day, "You diligently study the scriptures because you think by them you possess eternal life. These are the Scriptures that testify about me, yet you refuse to come to me to have life."[39] In other words, the point of the Scriptures is Jesus, not the Scriptures.[40] If you miss him, all the bible study ritual in the world is a waste of time. So read however you need to read. Just make sure you don't miss Jesus.

Another time in Jesus' ministry, he really gets angry at some folks for buying and selling in the temple, a place which was the poster child for ritual in its day. He gets so mad that he unleashes with a whip on the cattle to get them out of there, and he overturns some tables in the process. Then he delivers a slicing zing about his Father's house being a house of prayer but having been turned into a den of robbers.[41] At first glance it seems that Jesus is bothered at the commerce in the temple, which is why some folks used to get really bent out of shape if the youth group had a bake sale in the church foyer.

But closer inspection reveals more to the story. Jews in Jesus' day were commanded by Torah to offer sacrifices at the yearly feast of Passover. The wrinkle was that 80% of the people there at the annual feast were from out of town, which meant they had to bring their sacrifice, i.e., their goat, bull, lamb, birds, etc., with them. Now Leviticus 22 makes clear that any animal offered as a sacrifice to God must be pristine and without defect. And in Exodus, God says regarding this feast that no one is to come before him empty handed.[42]

So in Jesus' day, the religious establishment offered a service by providing animals for purchase by out-of-towners in case one of their own animals was not suitable after the journey. The problem was the animals brought by the out-of-towners had to be inspected per Leviticus 22.

If the animals in question were found to have defect, then their owners would be precluded from sacrificing, i.e., not allowed to worship at the temple. The implication is that they would not be allowed to keep Torah, unless of course, they wished to purchase a priest-approved animal on site at an exorbitant price. "No sir, I'm sorry, your lamb's just not going to cut it. Defects and blemishes all over the place. But we happen to have a (ridiculously expensive) lamb here for sale if you'd like to keep Torah and worship today...."

So the hapless Israelite was forced to buy an animal at an outrageous mark up. Then this: "Oh, I'm sorry, sir. We don't accept your out-of-region currency. You must first exchange it to the local currency. Of course, you'll take a beating on the exchange rate, but that's what it takes for you to keep the commands of Moses. Thanks so much for your business." So the out-of-towner takes a hit on the exchange to buy a pre-approved animal to give to the priest who will sacrifice part of it by roasting it over the fire, and eat the other part.

And *that* is why Jesus was furious and took the whip to the temple: it was, as it still is, about access, not commerce. They had confused the means with the end.

The problem with ritual is that it always carries with it the danger of becoming the point. Jesus was not furious about commerce in the Temple. He was furious about commerce in the Temple *being the point*. Because as soon as commerce in the Temple became the point of access to God, people who wanted to be in God's presence and do what he asked were denied. They no longer had access to God through the ritual. The ritual was keeping them from God, rather than bringing them to God.

A bit later Jesus celebrates the Passover feast with his disciples. And except for the new-theology-of-wine-and-bread, he did it just the way every Jew since the Exodus had done it, which is to say he followed the ritual of the meal. We know it as the Last Supper. But in that meal he stops the ritual of flashing back, and starts the ritual of flashing forward.[43] The meal takes on new theological depth and meaning, because the one preparing the meal is about to fulfill it to a thinner degree.[44] "Dear Disciples, *this* no longer means *that back there*. From now on, *this* means *that up ahead.*"

For McKee, the point is not the ritual of going to the theater. The theater is just the context, the tool to get him to the real point: *the truth as told by the motion picture story*. No one goes to the theater just to go to the theater and sit in a dark room with strangers. Mr. McKee has discovered—no doubt unwittingly—the same problem with ritual that plagued the Hebrews in the bible: making the ritual the point accomplishes exactly the opposite of what the ritual is trying to achieve in the first place. Because ritual always moves toward something larger. The minute it stops doing that, the ritual has become the end and not the means. That is unhealthy at best and theologically treacherous at worst. Just ask Martin Luther.

Instead of Church Camp, Jews in the New Testament world still kept all sorts of other religious ritual. By the time Jesus was on the scene, Jews contemporary with him distinguished themselves from the surrounding society by keeping kosher laws, keeping Sabbath, and circumcision. These rituals were the boundary markers of what made a Jew a Jew to the first-century world.[45] But through the writings of Paul in Romans and Galatians,[46] we see that these things were actually keeping those Jews from the very world God was asking them to engage.

Oh sure, they were separated. In the first century, there was no chance of anyone confusing a Jew with a, say, Joppan, or a Corinthian, or an Idumean. But, as mentioned earlier, God set aside a *chosen* people, not just to bestow upon them special favor, but to carry a message of the redemption of humanity, to be "a light to the nations," to use Isaiah's words.[47]

Jesus accomplished exactly this in the big theological sense (he was Jew, after all), but historically, someone had to pass his message along once he was taken to heaven forty days after the resurrection. The Jews would have been the obvious choice, but only some of them believed in Jesus and were therefore willing to put down the kosher/circumcision/Sabbath ritual. They did this because they saw the ritual for what it was, and more importantly what it was not.

Ritual is designed to be a means. When we turn ritual into the end, we elevate it to the place where the real end should be. We turn the ritual into a god. We expect the ritual to fulfill us, and sustain us, as Mr. McKee does every time he sits in a theater and the lights go down. I'm sure he's disappointed more often that not; when was the last movie you saw that elevated you to a higher place? Asking something so small to do a job so big is risky business.

(Short aside: This is probably why the movies that win the Best Picture Oscars are the ones that Normal Americans find strange and in some cases yucky. Because the Academy of Motion Picture Arts & Sciences is made up of actors, directors, producers, etc. Professional story tellers have spent so much time in the storytelling world, they see so many films and read so many scripts, that something has to be really out there to catch *those* people's attention. The rest of America just wants a good story where the good guy wins, the bad guy gets justice, love triumphs, and there's no cussing or naked people. Because to us, *those* are what make a good movie. Most of us don't even know what a cinematographer actually does. End of aside.)

So there are some who worship church, some who worship youth group, some who worship bible reading, some who worship mission work, some who worship camp, some who worship the worship conference, ad infinitum. These are meant to be the *how* we worship, never the *what*. We want the ritual to give us joy and hope and love. We long for the ritual, in some cases all year long, so that the ritual will give us the thing that will complete us. But it can never be so. Because the best ritual can do is provide a context, a launch pad to lead us to the One who *can* do all these things. As soon as we start expecting ritual to do it, the ritual will disappoint us, like when I got back to camp one year later and things just weren't the same.

All the singing and all the marshmallows and all the lessons and all the crafts and everything else about the Camp ritual are designed to show us God. And they will, but only if we look beyond them, and move toward that to which they are pointing. But was soon as we start to seek God *in* the singing, marshmallows, lessons, and crafts, the ritual will be found wanting. This was true of the sacrificial system in the Old Testament, and it's true today with our Christian rites.

Here are some passages to consider on this point. Hear the Psalmist's poignant lines:

Hear, O my people, and I will speak; O Israel, I will testify against you. I am God, your God. Not for your sacrifices do I rebuke you; your burnt offerings are continually before me. I will not accept a bull from your house or goats from your folds.   Psalm 50:7-9

"For since the law has but a shadow of the good things to come instead of the true form of these realities, it can never, by the same sacrifices that are continually offered every year, make perfect those who draw near. Otherwise, would they not have ceased to be offered, since the worshippers, having once been cleansed, would no longer have any consciousness of sins? But in these sacrifices there is a reminder of sins every year. For it is impossible for the blood of bulls and goats to take away sins. Consequently, when Christ came into the world, he said, "Sacrifices and offerings you have not desired, but a body have you prepared for me; in burnt offerings and sin offerings you have taken no pleasure. Then I said, 'Behold, I have come to do your will, O God, as it is written of me in the scroll of the book.'"   Hebrews 10:1-7

Or hear these words from the writer of Hebrews:

Or hear these words from the prophet and king-anointer Samuel:

> "Has the Lord as great delight in burnt offerings and sacrifices, as in obeying the voice of the Lord? Behold, to obey is better than sacrifice, and to listen than the fat of rams. For rebellion is as the sin of divination, and presumption is as iniquity and idolatry. Because you have rejected the word of the Lord, he has also rejected you from being king."   1 Sam. 15:22-23

Things get more intense when God speaks through the prophet Amos:

> "I hate, I despise your feasts, and I take no delight in your solemn assemblies. Even though you offer me your burnt offerings and grain offerings, I will not accept them; and the peace offerings of your fattened animals, I will not look upon them. Take away from me the noise of your songs; to the melody of your harps I will not listen. But let justice roll down like waters, and righteousness like an ever-flowing stream."   Amos 5:21-24

Finally, these succinct words from God through Hosea: "For I desire steadfast love[48] and not sacrifice, the knowledge of God rather than burnt offerings." Hosea 6:6

God didn't give us the ritual for his sake. He gave us the ritual for our sake, so that we could have a way to wrap our minds around being in his presence. That's what baptism, prayers, alms, and a host of other rites are really about. They are about always being in his presence, not the ritual. God commanded the sacrifices, remember. It's not that the sacrifices were wrong, per se. It was that the sacrifices had (have) a tendency to become an epic adventure in missing the point.

Moses led the Hebrews out of Egypt in the exodus, the greatest salvation event of its day. Then God came up with a way that this event was to be remembered and commemorated every single year: the Passover Feast. In conversation with that commemoration, Moses was instructed by God on the sacrificial system of worship: ritual in cultus. This is how Israel was to give honor and praise to her God for all time: *observe the ritual as gratitude for what has been.* But then he comes right down off Mt. Sinai and discovers part of the Hebrew nation caught in the act of spiritual adultery, i.e., cheating on God.

Moses is furious, and justifiably so, for corrupting the ritual and proceeding as if everything were holy is among the worst of blasphemies. Jesus's closing sentiments in the Sermon on the Mount are connected to this idea, and they are unnerving: "Many will say to me on that day, 'Lord, Lord, did we not prophesy in your name, and in your name did we not drive out many demons and perform many miracles?' And I will tell them plainly, 'I never knew you. Away from me you evildoers!'"[49] In other words: "Jesus, didn't we do all the right things in the right order?" And Jesus says in response: "Yes, and yet tragically we're strangers, you and me."

14   PRIMITIVE

There is a thin place I found on I-30 between Dallas and Texarkana. I passed a house of worship. The billboard that advertised it said "Adult Novelty Shop next eXXXit."

It made me zero in on the concept of idolatry: putting something in the place of God and worshipping *that*.[50] How many other types of gods out there vying for our time, attention, and money? The significance of the adultery metaphor in the bible hit me like a bolt. You see it mainly in the Prophets, but it's sprinkled elsewhere. Basically the metaphor goes like this: God's relationship to his people is like a husband's relationship to his wife. If there is physical infidelity or adultery in the human marriage, that is analogous to God's people going off and worshiping other gods, i.e., commit spiritual adultery.

So essentially, Commandment #1 ("You shall have no other gods before me") is the vertical equivalent of the horizontal Commandment #7 ("You shall not commit adultery"). The metaphor makes perhaps its most profound appearances in the books of Hosea and Ezekiel. This part I've known for a long time. It's a beautiful and poetic and tragic metaphor.

Humanity being what it is, the good, beautiful, noble, and virtuous always manage to be corrupted somewhere on the journey. That's how sin is. It has no creative power of its own, so it must take what is good and mar it. So somewhere along the way, long before I-30, sex stopped being what it should have been: a connective to God. And it started being what it never should have: a god itself.

The religion of worshipping *this* god has been around for thousands of years. In ancient circles, it went by the name "fertility cult" because the point was to offer sex as a sacrifice so that the gods would bless you with fertility: a cosmic sexual vending machine type of religion. Ancient Corinth boasted a temple of a thousand prostitutes. So, yeah. They were very "religious."

Which brings me back to the house of worship on I-30. The new layer, the thin place, I discovered as I drove past the eXXXit was this: What if that adult novelty shop is the contemporary house of worship for people who have made sex their god? What if that place is where they *observe* (note the irony) their religion? Probably they wouldn't frame it in those terms, but idolatry is a slippery slope. And I'm guessing people who frequent adult novelty shops don't want to be involved in heightened fertility, but this religion isn't picky about its goals. The goals are free to morph over time/cultures; in our day sex is offered in the hopes of getting something in return all the time.

No, in the contemporary version, the god of sex is not exclusive like the God of the bible. The sex god will accept anyone from anywhere and will allow them to worship other things at the same time. Some converts are faithful (read: "addicted"). Some people just visit every so often. Some people wander in out of curiosity and hang around longer than they should. Its churches are many: strip clubs, anywhere there's free wi-fi, late night cable, the smartphone in your pocket, your computer, *that* section of Netflix.

People can worship this god with greater frequency and ease than ever before. Hotel rooms offer access to worship with a remote control that often sits inches away from the Gideon Bible. And in that instance, how appropriate is the name *remote control*, because the one using it is certainly being controlled. Remotely. Often, on demand.

What if the porn industry is the modern seminary for this religion, the modern temple of a thousand prostitutes? To become ordained requires not internal transformation, but skin-level idealism. Its pastors constantly evangelize, hoping to win converts to their particular denomination (fetish), but exclusivity is vehemently discouraged; seminarians and their flock are encouraged to try anything on the grounds that there are no rules. Anyone with a camera phone can apply for amateur status although such applications are mostly for entertainment purposes, just to say they did it.

People are welcomed and enticed to this religion from all walks of life. Mechanics. Teachers. Ballerinas. Zookeepers. Bank tellers. Coffee shop patrons. Policemen. Attorneys. Window washers. Gary in Accounting. Stock boys. Valets. Sue, who stays home with the kids. Chefs. Farmers. People in Greenland. People in school. Students in class. Students in class right now. Old. Young. Too Young. The gospel message of this religion is simple: look at *this* and do *this*, and you'll feel good, because *feeling* rules the day here. If sex is the god, feeling is the unholy spirit.

There is not one holy book, but many, each espousing an alternate way to worship. There are icons and worship aids for every type of believer. Some worship aids are free and require minimal set up, others are quite expensive and extensive, but promise a richer experience, because it is the worship that is the most important thing, not the day-to-day living. And consequences? Psssh. There are no consequences. It's all about the moment, not the day-to-day living, Monday through Friday.

It's converted millions over the years and has legions of ardent if somewhat discreet followers. Some try to renounce their faith. And they are successful in their journey for a while. But the siren never stops singing, and eventually they come back hungrier than ever to be sated by hyper-sensuality.

As I was driving in the middle of this long thin place, the connections started to emerge as if out of the fog. This god is even okay if you use It[51] to achieve some other goal, i.e. worship some other god, such as the god of Achievement, the god of Status, the god of The Corporate Ladder, or the god of Commercial Success.[52]

While in Bible College, I knew a girl who was in the youth group of the church at which I was an intern. She graduated and started as a freshman at that same Bible College. It was there she stumbled upon a cousin of the Sex god: the god of Being In Love.

It was in the air.

By nineteen, she'd fallen head-over-heals for some dude, and everyone knew it was a train wreck waiting to happen, but of course she wouldn't listen. Oh, she was in love. But she wasn't in love with the guy. She was in love with being in love. A year later I ran into her at the local grocery store. She no longer wore a wedding ring. And she was pushing a three-month old. She had very tired eyes, and shoulders, and soul. She'd aged a decade in the twelve months since I'd seen her. She had the look and feel of a person who had, in a heartbreaking way, discovered their worldview had been built on a house of cards.

A few miles farther down I-30, I was struck by this: What if there are other modern gods that people worship nowadays, in the same way the (so-called) primitive polytheistic pagans did in the ancient world?

How about the god of News, its followers self-proclaimed "news junkies?" Adherents include those who constantly must be connected to information; 24-hour news rooms, texting gossip, checking scores and stock updates. People who are constantly surrounded by chatter. Their idea of hell is camping, or any place else off the grid.

The goddess of Fermentation? She is a cleverer god than most: she'll mess with your mind and then call you crazy for calling her on it. Country artist Brad Paisley even sings a song in which alcohol is personified, and she causes people to do all sorts of things we'd just as soon not remember.

The god of—can I say this?—Facebook? Of social media? No, Facebook is just the church. This is the god of Validation. These followers long to be spoken to in a kind or sincere way, to know that their ideas, pictures, and quotes matter, to know that their opinions count. Not a few teens would have their cell phones surgically grafted to their wrist if they could because they long for the validation that comes via tweets, Instaposts, and snapchats. I once overheard a kid at the school where I taught say this: "It's like the worst thing ever to see no new notifications."

For older folks, perhaps it's the god of Mattering...to culture, to their kids, to society, to old classmates, to long lost loves, and now to their caregivers. But they're wading in the world of the guarded surface. There are many positives to Facebook, but the trouble comes when people retreat to a false self, a shell, a virtual doppelgänger that is cooler and more wonderful and hotter. When social media becomes personal branding, we're in trouble.

Why? Why this overwhelmingly powerful drive to be connected constantly and validated for our postings? Could it be that God build into our soul's DNA a drive to live in and be in community? If we don't get it from the proper place, we will get it from somewhere, proper or not. This is why Facebook took off. In many ways it's a façade of self-commecialism, for sure, but it's community nonetheless.

Could that last sentence apply to your church? Or your friend group? Or your class? Or your collegues? Or do you find *real* community in those places? Just asking the question.

The ancient Egyptians and Aztecs both worshipped a god of the sun, and we look down our noses at their primitive belief system and their bizarre polytheism. But in our day, we have the god of the Earth. The god of the Environment. The god of the Climate, with Al Gore its high priest. As I said, everyone believes in something. We are made to worship, and when the God of the bible becomes a useless and obsolete abstraction, the soul searches and latches onto something else to worship: whatever it can find that fits the bill of The Greater Cause.

A quick poetic interlude, dedicated to Mr. Gore:

I Am Not Green
By Duncan Campbell

I rocket from the convenient store, squealing the tires
in my SUV, gas nozzle dripping on the ground
I hustle down to McDonald's
for a triple quarter-pounder

in one of the old styrofoam boxes.
I eat it by the river while texting,
then throw the box in the river
where a dolphin eats it
and chokes on it
and is struck by an oil tanker
which runs aground.
Oil rivers out
onto ducks and cattails.
The oil snares them.
I laugh at the ducks
because they deserve it.
Their webbed feet are caught in the
plastic web of my life and my six-pack container
from the convenient store
which I also threw in the river.
That was one good cheeseburger.

Hopefully you're chuckling at that because you instantly see how silly it is. But if that little bit of satirical poetry feels a bit abrasive, could it be because you've got a little god of Going Green in your closet?

The god of Being Right? (Just a word to the ladies here. You don't have to win every conversation. In fact, some of them you should lose on purpose. Yes, you're better at verbal communication than we are. We get it. Please don't use your aptitude to put us in a head lock. Then we lose motivation because we'd rather not do something that do it wrong.)

If the preceding paragraph raised your blood pressure a few ticks…did the god of Sexism start beeping on your radar?

The god of A Ripped Physique? (A word to the gents here. Suppose you put yourself through three years of egg white omelets, no sugar, and three hours at the gym every day. And suppose you are actually one of the lucky ones to have the genes to get a ripped physique, because not everyone can. And you get that ripped physique. You go to the beach, and take your shirt off. People ogle. Girls whisper. Some of them might even talk to you. But at the end of the day, you have to put your shirt on and leave because Monday you have to go back to work. And you just spent three years of your life dedicated to something that lasted a few hours. Any real woman who would give you longer than a few minutes would see you for what you are: a narcissist. Or suppose your goal is to be an actor and be The Hot Guy. Suppose you actually do a screen test and the director loves you. You will be on screen for at most fifteen seconds, because you are not an actor who portrays a role. You didn't take acting classes, you were at the gym. You are eye meat. And now you've given all that time in the gym for fifteen seconds of fame, and you *still* have to go to work on Monday, because people cast for fifteen seconds with no lines don't get paid very much.)

The god of a 4.0 GPA?

The god of Fair-Trade-Grass-Fed-Whole-Grain-Organic-ness?

The gods of Fortune and Destiny? Those gods are ever-popular today, but they actually originated in the Ancient Near East. This is from the book of Isaiah, who is speaking on God's behalf to those who abandoned him:

But as for you who forsake the Lord and forget my holy mountain, who spread a table for Fortune and fill bowls of mixed wine for Destiny, I will destine you to the sword, and you will all bend down for the slaughter; for I called you but you did not answer, I spoke but you did not listen. You did evil in my sight and chose what displeases me.

-Isaiah 65:11

So God feels pretty strongly about other gods. This should come as no surprise, given what he said on top of the "holy mountain" alluded to in this verse. Commandment number one is "You shall have no other gods before me."[53]

There are boatloads of others; the deities are endless. All this boils down to this one point: I want to stop confusing worshipping the creation with worshipping the Creator. The two are not the same. Everybody believes in something. The belief is not the problem. That part is primitively easy. It's the *something* that keeps giving me trouble.

ACT III

HORIZON

When you grow up by the sea, you spend a good deal of time looking at the horizon. You wonder what on Earth the waves might bring—and where the sea might deposit you—until one day you know you have lived between two places, the scene of arrival and the point of departure.

—Andrew O'Hagan

Bring me that horizon.

—Jack Sparrow

15 MESSY CALCULUS

Here is a wonderful tidbit from a delightfully thick book: "The Lord does not uphold moral order in a tidy equation where righteousness is immediately rewarded and evil is immediately punished. If that were the case, people would confuse pleasure with morality. People would behave righteously but for selfish reasons."[54]

Meaning: What if every time you did the right thing, you got some sort of reward? Like $40, or clean laundry, or no more bills that month, or a Ferrari? And what if every time you did the wrong thing, you got your fingers smashed in the door, or you got audited, or you lost your wallet, or you gained six pounds?

If this were the way the world worked, then pretty soon, people would be doing the right thing because they wanted the reward instead of because it was right. They would worship the god of Being Righteous. Likewise, they would avoid wrong not on the basis of it being wrong, but on the basis of not wanting to gain six pounds or get a visit from the IRS.

So God had to figure out a way to guarantee that when people did the right thing, it would be for selfless and noble purposes.[55] Until late one night God sat bolt upright in bed and thundered "I GOT IT! I'll make reality such that righteousness isn't always rewarded! Sometimes they'll do the right thing, and I'll make it so no one sees them! Wait, even better: sometimes they'll do the right thing and they'll *still* get mugged by goons in a back alley! WAIT A SECOND! Sometimes I'll let the bad guys get away with it for the time being! This is perfect!" And so it was.

Isn't that how you feel sometimes? Like you just can't get ahead, no matter how many times you do the right thing? Like you choose to do the right thing, and all of a sudden life gets, excuse me, *harder?* What is that all about?

But pain is not necessarily punishment. Sometimes it is. Other times, pain just *is*, and there's no explaining it. Maybe the problem isn't the problem. Maybe the problem is our expectations of the resolution. Sometimes the discomfort, the twinge, the pull, the twist, the bind, and the tension is the opportunity to realize and acknowledge your lesser-ness. Your need. Your I-Must-Rely-On-Something-Else-ness.

Sometimes in the grinder is where the greatness lies. But it's not very fun, or sexy, or the kind of thing you talk about over coffee. It's the grinder, after all.

The trouble is we all want the daisies and strawberries. But those are not what impel us to grow, drive us upward, force us to our knees. But like your muscles, neither will our souls grow unless they are taxed to lift more than they are able. Eventually the muscle can no longer lift the weight, and the weight clanks to the floor, dropped in exhaustion.

The muscle is sore for a few days, because its fibers have been shredded by an unreasonable amount of strain. But then it uses some protein, some carbs, some electrolytes, and it starts to rebuild, bigger and stronger than what it was before. More sleek. Able to lift more the next time. So it is with the spirit, who feeds not on carbs, but nearness, and rebuilds not with protein but prayer.

It is a heartbreaking truth that God sometimes has to break our hearts to get our attention. Sometimes he's in the earthquaking mountain fireball of terror (Exodus 19). Sometimes he's in the whisper (1 Kings 19). But the mode is not nearly as important as the fact that he is there with us, salving our souls with his presence and words, as any good parent does.

One Sunday at worship, our youngest son Sam (eleven months old at the time) initiated a rousing game of peek-a-boo with the twenty-something girl sitting behind us. He started to hide behind his mama, who was holding him, then popped out and batted his blue eyes at the girl, who of course was melting at this. And it was fun to watch, and slightly awkward because all this was happening during the sermon; every so often a serious point was punctuated with a giggle from the back. We were *that* family.

But an important developmental milestone had taken place: that of Object Permanence. This means that our son had reached the stage where he was able to conceptualize that just because he can't see the girl in the row behind, she's still very much there.

Before this stage, when mama or daddy left the room, in his mind, they were gone forever; not being able to see them equaled absence. But once a child hits Object Permanence, he has achieved a higher-level thinking which then allows for the child to be comfortable even when they can't see mom or dad. They have come to know that even though dad might not be in the room at the moment, dad still exists. He may not be with me right now, but he's still with me.

This also allows for the joy of being surprised, which is exactly what I did earlier tonight with Sam. He was sitting in the middle of our bed, and I would come stomping around the corner like a rhino and making a silly face. He would giggle like crazy at this new, exciting game. Then I would leave for a few seconds, and we'd do it all over again. It was a joyous moment of our relationship, whereas before, my leaving the room would not have produced anticipation but sheer terror.

And I wonder if perhaps there is a spiritual equivalent to Object Permanence: a developmental place of faith to which we should aspire that allows us to believe with certainty that God has not left us even though he may not be visible at the moment, a place where we no longer say, "Oh look, it's raining, therefore the sun doesn't exist."

Because the truth is that he is here, and he has not left us, and he is at work, and he does enjoy time with us not because of what we do but because of what we are: his children. What changes is our view, recognition, posture, and perspective. If we cannot see him, perhaps it's our eyes that are the problem. Perhaps he's present in a way other than what eyes can see.

"Emmanuel" in Matthew 1:23 means *God with us*. And the last words Jesus ever spoke before he ascended to heaven were "and I am with you always" (Matthew 28:20). Between those two verses are the story of a God who came down to be with us in the midst of our pain, to be next to us, to be near, near enough to feel the breath of him, near enough to feel His Spirit. He is to be just on the other side of the veil, hidden, yes, but ever-near. Permanently.

16   APOLLO 13

What if you had this really important thing to say to an ant? Like, say, where the lifetime supply of fresh cut watermelon is. How in the world would you communicate it? You'd have to stoop really low, first of all. Then you'd have to convince the ant not to be terrified of you, you being 6,000 times his size, and very loud. Then you'd have to figure out some way to get the ant to stay still long enough to listen to you.

Then you'd have to learn to speak ant language, which is probably a language of smells more than anything. Then you'd have to come up with a way to translate your idea from your language, which is verbal, to ant language, which is olfactory. Then, once you got your verbal idea into olfactory language, you would still have to convince the ant you're trustworthy, that you're really not luring him to a can of Raid instead.

This is exhausting. And it's all for *one idea.*

I used to get so frustrated with John the Professor when I was in grad school because he only taught part time at the campus where I was. Every class he taught was a treasure trove of thin places. I really wished he would have taught more classes to us high-ups. But no, his full time teaching gig was teaching

Intro to Bible to freshmen over at Bible Undergraduate College, people on whom his brilliance was obviously lost.

Here I was trying to understand God, and the undergrads were playing solitaire—*solitaire!*—during his lectures. When someone told me that, I wanted to march straight into the lecture hall and stick a fork in the outlet and fry all their hard drives. I brooded over this for entirely too long.

Then it hit me one day that he was in the noblest post. Sure, they didn't get it all the time. Sure, it would be professionally gratifying to be able to begin sentences with "When I teach Ph.D. candidates…" but he wasn't interested in any of that. He was more interested in taking ideas and concepts and languages that maybe two thousand people on the planet could read and conceptualize, and bringing them down to eighteen-year-old level. That shot a sizable hole in my smugness and taught me a painful lesson in Jesus-level humility

This is precisely why you may discover a thin place at Isaiah 1:18 if you stare at it long enough. In it, God says, "Come now, let us reason together." Most people, when they encounter Isaiah 1:18, they concentrate on the back half of the verse, which talks about sins being washed away white as snow. Of course this is important, and not a little thin itself. But for the moment, flex your theological curiosity muscle and hone in on the first part of the verse. The almighty Creator of everything, the One who thought of the universe and then spoke it into existence, wants to have a conversation with you. He who invented quantum physics, gave Shakespeare his ink, and engineered human history, wants to talk some things through.

With us.

With us, who eeked out a C in algebra. We, who forgot to take out the trash this morning. We, who haven't the first clue about how our cars' camshafts work, and we, who laugh when the guy on the beer commercial gets hit in groin.

We have our moments of brilliance, for sure, but they are few and far between. Most of the time we're just trying to figure things out with limited resources, to put the puzzle together with only half the picture as a reference.

There's a sequence like this in *Apollo 13,* when the air tanks explode, leaving Tom Hanks and his two buddies in a rapidly-depleting oxygen situation. There is a solution though: to replace the oxygen filers in one module with the filters from the other. But there's a problem (of course). The command module's oxygen filters are round, but the lunar module's filters are cube-shaped. So this complicates things. And the clock is ticking; the astronauts are hours away from brain asphyxia, and they have no idea how to proceed. It's not a contingency they've even remotely considered.

So the guys back in Houston dump a big box of stuff on the table, and one guy picks up one of each filter and says, "The people upstairs have handed us this one and we gotta come through. We gotta make *this* (cube filter) fit into a hole made for *this* (round filter) using nothing but *that.*"[56] And he points to the stuff on the table from the box. And they all get to work.

This is a brilliant picture of Jesus.

Because down on earth there are a thousand solutions to the problem. Back at mission control, they could calculate, invent, create and slide-rule (we're in the 70's, remember) their way to fixing the cube-filter-in-a-round-hole problem. But 99% of those solutions are useless, *because the guys in space don't have access to those 99% of solutions.* The guys in Houston can only use what's in the box, because what's in the box is only the inventory of supplies the guys have in space.

And Jesus, the God-Man, comes down here and could've done all kinds of things to tell us and show us his message. He could have spoken in color. He could've sung the Himalayas. He could have clairvoyant-ed it to us. Or he could have explained about DNA and the stratosphere and what a sacrifice bunt is. But he didn't because 99% of those things wouldn't communicate to his audience.

Instead, he opts for the simple imagery and metaphors everyone in his time can understand because it was common to them. So he tells stories of fish, and sheep, and coins, and mustard seeds, and lamps, and bread. And that was *once he got down here.* Coming down to earth, incarnating, enfleshing in the first place was the gargantuan step in the direction of a solution. He put Himself in a box and dumped it on the table, and said, *"We gotta make this (God's infinite love) fit into this (our brains) using nothing but that (sower, mustard seeds, oil, pearls, etc.)."* And then he got to work.

Because there is a sense in which Jesus came to communicate the thin places to us and point them out. He came to give us a glimpse of God, to show us God's character, to paint for us God's image.[57] But there is also a sense in which Jesus is the thin place. When people were with him, they didn't just experience the God out there. They experienced the God down here who was at once here, but was one with the One there.[58] And that's only the beginning of the paradoxes.

If you are to be first (goal), you must be last (tool). Making yourself last for last's sake is torturous because it robs you of hope and makes you feel guilty for not liking being last. If you are to find comfort (goal), you must mourn (tool). If suffering and sadness and hurt over sin just hangs around and doesn't *do* anything except make you blue, then it is a catastrophic waste. The darkness is supposed to lead you, or better, drive you somewhere. For some it is just darkness, but it can be a summons toward light.

To the modern Western (read: Enlightement-influenced) mind, paradoxes are a hassle. Our default is Find an Easier Way, which is too bad because somewhere along the line we swallowed the lie that the easiest road is the best road. I think most people start thinking this way in junior high because that's when homework really amps up; you really start to figure out the quickest way to just get it done, whether the actual lessons are learned or not. This starts a pattern that leads to high school and college, and if you're not careful, a life culture. Even if we have the mental chops to do the gymnastics, mostly our first impulse is to watch tv.

Jesus will have none of that. Laziness has no place in the walk of a disciple, then or now. His is a road that is often times intentionally difficult. But then Jesus knows the truth that it is the hardness that drives us to God, not the cushiness. Had Jesus had homework, his primary goal would have been to learn, not just to do homework for homework's sake. Making homework the point, misses the real point, which is to learn by experience. The first step in sorting out homework, or any progress for that matter, is to figure out the difference between the goal and the tool.

Which is the goal and which is the tool? Here, you try:

To be wise with your money is to give it away.
If you are to find your life, you must lose it.
Being selfless is the only way truly to get what you need.

Make the wrong one the goal, and you look like a fool. Make the right one the goal and you look like Jesus. There are far too many of these for them to be the result of some cosmic coincidence. They point to something deeper, something richer that we find in this life only when we stop looking. Jesus knew this, which he tried so hard to tell us ants.

17 BROTHERS

My wife and I had just had our second child, a son as well. We were still staying in the hospital that night, and I was lying on the roll-away cot the nurses had brought in for me. Our first son was staying at our house with his grandma, so in the hospital room, it was just my wife and I and the newborn. The birth wasn't as surreal to me as when our first was born, but it was still pretty incredible. For one thing, I apparently married Superwoman, because we went from Hospital-Check-In to Holding-Our-Newborn in three hours. But the other amazing part for me happened after the fact, that night, when all the lights were off. I was thinking of the all the new wrinkles to all the new relationships that were about to happen in our family, specifically how my relationship with my firstborn would change.

The days have long since started when God teaches me about Himself by using my first son; all the Father/Son ideas, concepts, experiences had been brought to bear in my own life. That's been happening for a while now. And I'd find myself frustrated first, but then in awe when Humphrey, our first, ignored me. Or when he hugged me. Or when we played. Or when he discovered something I was trying to teach him. Going through those things as a father is wonderful, yes, but it also eye-opening and transparent. Every time I say something like, "If you'd just listened to dad the first time, it would have taken a lot less time and been a lot easier…" or "You can't treat your brother that way…" or "Ok, but there are other things that are more important that you have to do first…", I hear God winking at me, and most times I cringe because those lines could be his very words to me.

In Humphrey's mind, his world is simply right there in that moment, but I'm right next to him, going through the exact same experience. I see it from the father perspective, sensing a thin place at every turn, because I'm seeing my experience with him and equating it, at least in some rudimentary way, with God's experiences with me. Up until Humphrey was born, I was the son in the Father/child relationship metaphor with God. I still am, I suppose, but now there is the added dimension of my discovering what it's like to be the father to a son. It is terrifying and holy to discover these things, which makes sense because God is terrifying and holy.

I can warn my son. I can foresee danger. I know what brings him joy. I memorize his mannerisms. I stand by him when he won't stay in bed. I let consequences play out. I spoil him (sometimes). I look out for him in parking lots. But I now have a depth and texture to my understanding of God that I didn't have before I had a son, because if I can feel all those things toward my son, God must be able to feel them with me, on an infinitely larger scale. And of course God wants me to teach my son about Him. But that's not why God gave Humphrey to me. I'm convinced He gave Humphrey to me so that God could teach me about Himself. And I just have three children. He's got millions of sons and daughters.

Which brings me back to the hospital.

I was laying awake in the cot, thinking about the thin places God must have in store for me now that I had *two* whole sons. I found a thin place right there in room 272 of St. Francis Hospital. It hit me that my relationship with Sam, my second-born, is not the only place Sam will know me. Sooner or later, Sam's going to ask his big brother about me. He will learn about who I am, about his father, *through his brother*.

How will Humphrey describe me to Sam, or to any other children we have? The implications of this are astounding. I mean, I'm the father, fully capable of explaining myself to Sam or Humphrey or anyone else for that matter. But I won't always get asked. At some point one of my sons will ask the other one what I'll think, or how I'll respond, or whether I'll give my support, or what I'll do. And regardless of the truth, what will be communicated between sons, in son-language, will be totally based on the answering son's experience.

So I must form, build, fashion, and carve out a my relationship with Humphrey such that he can express it to others truthfully and accurately using his own language and ideas. Because if Sam says, "Who is that man who sleeps in the bed with Mama?" and Humphrey responds, "Him? That's dad." And Sam says, "What's Dad like?" and Humphrey responds, "He plays golf a lot and cooks on the grill," then in a very large sense, I have missed the boat. Not that it would be wrong, per se, to be so described; I do play golf and I do grill out. But that's not what I want to be known for among sons. What I want Humphrey to say to his brother is something like, "He's the one who protects us, and prays for us and carries us when we ask," or "He's the one who makes sure we have food to eat and plays roughhouse with us."

But unless I set about the business of protecting, praying, carrying, providing, and playing roughhouse, there's absolutely no way Humphrey could respond that way. It won't even be in his box of possible answers. So there is now a mighty—and I would argue holy—impetus on me to give Humphrey something good to say to his brother. Not just good. Something meaningful, powerful, righteous, clever, faithful, and holy. In some sense, how we are described by our children to their siblings is a very acute measure of our deepest character.

As it turns out, Humphrey did just that. Humphrey was seven when I decided to test my theory. I had just gotten home from a conference in Houston. It was late, and he was in bed. I asked Humphrey: "If your brother were just born and he came home from the hospital, but he was born at the same age he is now (3½), and I was still in Houston when y'all got home, and he asked you about me, what would you say?"

Humphrey looked at me, thinking. "Hmmm. I'd say 'Dad is friendly and tall. He's got long arms and brown hair and hazel eyes and his lips aren't that pink and he hasn't shaved in a while and he wears jeans a lot and he works and helps mom and he loves you.'"

"If your brother asked you 'How do I know dad loves me,' how would you answer?"

"I'd say 'He's dad. You'll just know.'"

sigh If you saw a glow from the west that night, it was my heart.

But what if Sam weren't my son yet? What if Sam were just some kid who came to live with us, and it was ultimately his decision whether or not he would become part of our family? And what if I didn't talk? What if the *only* way Sam would make a decision about whether our family was worth joining was based on what Humphrey said to him? Would Humphrey's experience with me, and his explanation of it, be enough to convince Sam to let himself be adopted? I sure hope so.

To make matters more complicated, now we've got a daughter, Ilsa, thrown into the mix. What if she were to become the "third-generation dad learner?" What if the only things she could know about me are what Sam could tell her? How accurate would that be, transmitting his knowledge/experience after having been taught by Humphrey? What if he missed something? What if he's not a good teacher? What if he's a really good teacher but decides to add in stuff he made up, like I wear sweaters in June and only drink goat milk (I don't.) What would be the most important, and what would get lost in translation? I get the picture that somewhere God is saying to us #thestruggleisreal.

God's family is now one of adoption.[59] One doesn't "get in" by birth anymore. One "gets in" by faith, in its various expressions.[60] What is incredible is that He doesn't come to us individually, speaking to us in an audible voice, and telling every truth and fact we've always wanted to know. Instead, He remains audibly silent, choosing instead to speak only through his Word and the lives of his people. He stakes his reputation on his adopted children. This is surely a messy way to do things, because it takes an incredible amount of faith to believe in God after seeing what some his knuckle-headed children do, and do to each other. On the other hand, if God met you at the breakfast table, poured some coffee, and explained everything in crystal-clear terms...well, that wouldn't take much faith to believe, would it?

For God has many children who are in special, divine, loving, forgiven relationships with him. And since God chooses no longer to speak in an audible voice,[61] those children are forever trying to convince others to become his children. In a sense, they become God's voice via the Holy Spirit inside them. And what they must convey, in son/daughter-language, is the truth of who God is in real, honest, truthful, yet accurate ways. Yes, sometimes the children get it wrong because they don't have all the facts or they have misinterpreted, or they don't know all the story or they just haven't had much experience with God yet. But sometimes the children get it dead right because they have been touched in such a way that their lives now profess the truth of the tremendous God they serve.

They have found redemption, peace, and an indescribable love, and they are weary of holding it in, indeed they cannot. The outflowing, the explosion of God from their lives is the most powerful witness there is to the rest of world. In a market place of faith, where sex gods, fortunes, and pseudo-selves are very viable and prevalent options, the draw of a God-touched life is undeniable. For out of the fog and bedlam of our world and all she has to offer, there comes a voice, the voice of a God-touched life. And it will be no louder than the other voices, for it's not the volume that is compelling; it's the source. And the voice says, "There's more. There's more to it that this."

18   DESMOND THE MIGHTY

Once upon a time, at the school where I used to teach, there was a young man named Desmond. He was handsome, charismatic, kind, and was well-built and all that. One day in chapel, Desmond went on stage and approached a long, thick rope tethered to a large object which was covered by a canvas. It was large and flat, about the size of a ping-pong table, and very, very heavy. Desmond couldn't see the what was under the cover or where the rope was tied; no one could. Only the old man knew what was under the cover. And the old man spoke to Desmond, "I'd like you to pull on the rope attached to that object. Can you do that?"

"Yes," Desmond replied, and Desmond just knew that he could. He was very strong, and he liked this idea. "No matter what happens, just keep pulling," said the old man. "You can do it."

So Desmond started to pull. But not with all his might yet. He was testing the waters. "Why give 100% when 40% will do?" he supposed. So pull at 40% he did.

Exactly nothing happened. But Desmond steeled his resolve. "Perhaps pulling at 70% of my strength would move the object," thought he. So he gripped the rope anew and began to pull with two-thirds of his considerable strength. And nothing.

Zilch. Zero. Desmond the Mighty became frustrated. Over five hundred people were in the audience watching him fail. He was Mighty. He was not accustomed to this.

The old man, sensing the mood starting to ebb, turned to the audience. "Maybe you all are not cheering loud enough," said he. And so the audience of Desmond's classmates and underclassmen started to holler, yell, hoot, cheer, raise the roof, hail, clap, and encourage Desmond the Mighty. And Desmond was boosted, so he pulled harder still.

And still, nothing.

Desmond started to slacken the rope, and it bowed downward before him like an upside down rainbow, his hands atingle with the burn of jute against flesh.

"Would you like some help?" the old man asked. Desmond's forehead was glistening.

"Yes."

The old man surveyed the audience, and found many raising their hands to volunteer their strength. But he called none of them. Instead he turned back to Desmond the Mighty and produced from a box some thick leather gloves, which he happily handed to Desmond. Desmond deflated a bit, thinking the old man was going to send another person. But he donned the gloves with a grateful smile nonetheless. "Thank you," said he, then resumed his pulling, but with considerably less enthusiasm.

"You're doing great," said the old man.

"Is that object bolted to the ground?" queried Desmond.

"No. It is not. Are you tired?"

"Yes."

"That's okay. Keep pulling."

So Desmond the Mighty pulled on. And still the object didn't move. Not even an inch. It didn't even wiggle.

"Can I please have another person to help me?" asked Desmond, his shirt quite moist now.

"Another person? Are you sure? You're doing fine."

"Please?"

The old man turned back to the audience. More hands shot into the air. The old man selected Meredith the Seventh Grader, who was neither muscular nor large. In fact, she was quite tiny.

This was not was Desmond was expecting, but he was grateful for the help all the same. So Desmond the Mighty and Meredith the Seventh Grader introduced themselves, never having met—why would they?—and started to pull together. And pulled. And pulled. And pulled. Try as they might, the object never moved.

"Is this a trick?" said the girl.

"No," replied the old man.

"Can we move it?" said she.

"Sure, if you pull hard enough," said he.

So they regrouped, huddled, and formed a new plan. They renewed their strength, counted to three, took a running start, and gave a mighty yank. And nothing. Not even the tiniest of quivers. Frustration was starting to creep back in. Desmond crawled through the loop in the end of the rope and got inside it, creeping on all fours with all his might while Meredith, now wearing the gloves, pulled with all her might, too

They exhausted their efforts and themselves. So they stopped.

"Keep pulling," said the old man.

"Why?" said Desmond, a little more apathy in his inflection than perhaps he'd intended.

"Because I asked you to," said the old man, maddeningly calm.

"Can we have more help?" asked Desmond, politely, if out of breath.

"Why? You're doing fine," replied the old man.

"Please?"

The old man turned back to the audience, and this time selected Maya the Ninth Grade Volleyball Player and Cody the Football Player, who galloped up on stage and grabbed the rope in between Desmond and the Meredith the Seventh Grader. All plans foregone, this was now about strength: theirs vs. the object's. They would not be defeated. They would not be turned away. They would conquer the object. It was a matter of principle now. And they all pulled, and pulled, and pulled as hard as they could, until faces reddened and veins popped out of necks.

And the object moved. About two feet.

A raucous cheer bellowed in the hall; yells and claps erupted for the four heroes, who finally succeeded in moving the object. On stage, they hi-fived each other and hugged, the dragon now slain.

They all walked—no, *strutted*—off stage and returned to their seats, except for Desmond the Mighty. He was drenched in sweat and barely able to stand at then end of his journey. The old man summoned him. He came.

"Desmond, I'm proud of you."

"Thank you."

"What did you learn?"

"We can't do it alone. We have to work together to move heavy objects. We have to work together to succeed. Otherwise we fail."

The crowd applauded once again.

"Yes, that's true. But Desmond," said the old man, his voice growing very quiet now, intimate, even.

"You never failed. You were a success *before* it ever moved."

Desmond the Mighty looked quizzically at the old man. The audience leaned in.

"You did exactly what I asked, Desmond. You kept pulling. I never asked you to move the object, only to pull. Moving it was your plan and your idea, and if I may say, it was far more difficult than my plan. My plan was for you to keep pulling, no matter what happened. I gave you the gloves because they helped you do the task I set before you, even though you were disappointed when I gave them to you. The extra people were helpful, but only for your goal, not mine. But you did well. You pulled until the very end. Well done."

Then the bell rang and everyone stood to leave chapel, and Desmond headed back to the land of high school, which was a difficult land, requiring much pulling.

19 THERMAL DEATH POINT

Bread.

Just saying the word probably evokes a memory of a smell, a meal with someone special, a favorite recipe. What is it about it? It's the classic food. And for good reason. It's 30,000 years old.[62]

I'm no chef, but I know there are at least 148 different kinds of bread. Every culture and people group on earth have some form of bread. They may not each eat it every day, but it's in their cultural recipe book. It is universal. It is a staple. And it is good.

And here's what's crazy: all of those breads—and I'd venture to say the unknown ones too—are basically made with five things. Flour. Water. Salt. Leavening. Heat. That's it. Now the flour may be wheat, rye, corn, or rice, or some other kind. The water might be in milk. The salt might come from butter. Although most have it, the leavening is optional—just ask Moses. But it can be yeast, beer, baking soda, mineral water, yogurt, or egg whites. And the dough can be baked at a variety of temperatures for a variety of lengths of time.

To change the proportions of any or all of those five elements will alter the entire final product drastically. *And they will all be good.* I defy anyone not to smile when they smell ciabatta baking, even those of you who do the gluten-free thing. Some of the best bread I have ever had was at an outdoor market in Helsinki, Finland, right on the water. My buddies and I took one bite, along with the salmon they cooked on the spot, and none of us said anything. We all just looked at each other and chewed and smiled. It was so good, in fact, that I returned there eight months later with my future wife and ate the same bread. It was even better.

Because bread just has this…flavor. You can't quantify it, except in levels of "Oh man, you GOTTA try this," or "WOW, that smells AMAZING!" or, even better, silence and inhales and knowing. I don't believe that comes only from the skilled hands of a baker. I think it's much deeper. On some level, all food is transformational; there's this thing, and it radically changes into this other thing.

But bread…bread is special. Because bread makes the biggest journey of all. From life to death, and back again. Several times, in fact. Bread starts out as a grain. Wheat, let's say. So some farmer plants his wheat. No, he plants a seed. A seed that has the potential for life. But unless that seed dies underground and splits open, it will never realize its potential. In fact, Jesus said as much in John 12:24 ("Very truly I tell you, unless a kernel of wheat falls to the ground and dies, it remains only a single seed. But if it dies, it produces many seeds.").

So the wheat starts to grow because it's alive and that's what living things do. Time goes by. Then out come the combine harvesters. Or scythes, if you live in certain parts of the world. And all that wheat, all that alive-ness, is chopped down dead. We call this "harvest." But let's be honest; it's killing. Because in order to get the seeds, the plant has to die. Now some of the seeds that have the potential for future life can be saved, replanted, or passed on.

Or they can be crushed dead. Into flour. Once that happens, all of their future life-giving potential ceases.

Unless you change what you mean by "life."

So now there's this five-pound bag of flour at the grocery store. We take it home. We add some water. We add some salt. We mix it together, and we create, in culinary terms, "clay." It's dough. But it's like clay. And to that clay, we add some "leaven." Leaven comes from the root word that means enliven: to vivify, to bring to life. And the Hebrew word for clay? Adam. As in the first man, as in God breathed into clay and made Adam.[63] And now our dough, while it's not an intelligent life form, is now very much alive. It must be, for it is growing, and growth is the proof of life. Listen to chef Peter Reinhart explain:[64]

> And while it's growing, all these literal transformations are taking place. Enzymes are breaking down sugars. Yeast is eating sugar and turning it into carbon dioxide and alcohol. Bacteria is in there, eating the same sugars, turning them into acids. In other words, personality and character is being developed in this dough under the watchful gaze of the baker. And the baker's choices all along the way determine the outcome of the product. A subtle change in temperature, a subtle change in time; it's all about a balancing act between time, temperature and ingredients. That's the art of baking.

Baking? That's the art of life. Reinhart again:[65]

But it's still just dough. As soon as the interior temperature of that dough crosses the threshold of 140 degrees, it passes what we call the "thermal death point." All life ceases there. The yeast, whose mission it has been up till now to raise the dough, to enliven it, to vivify it, in order to complete its mission, which is also to turn this dough into bread, has to give up its life.

And so it does. But in so doing, it creates what we call the staff of life. What goes in live dough comes out dead bread. It has been transformed. Again.

It is what all cultures eat. It is the universal staple. It is why it is so hard *not* to eat. Not eating it breaks the chain of transformation. If we leave it there in the loaf stage, it will just turn moldy and rot. Ah, but if we eat it...it will be alive again; it will enliven, vivify. All it has to do is hit your tongue. We ingest what will ultimately fuel us and give us life. We make a memory. We break bread with someone we love. We are full. For a while.

Jesus has other ideas. And he picks the mother of all object lessons to share them. At this point in his story, he has started to become popular. His teaching, if not his healing, has garnered the attention of the people. Lots of them. And he's gained a following. And this following finds themselves on the far shore of the Sea of Galilee with Jesus. The time of the Passover is near, John tells us, invoking our memory of the fateful night of the Exodus. God had told his children to eat roast lamb, bitter herbs, and bread baked without yeast. They were going to have to leave in a hurry and couldn't be bothered with waiting on the bread to rise. It became part of their tradition, their cultural identity. Passed down to Jesus's time.

Jesus notices the throng. He might have cocked an eyebrow at Philip. "How do you suppose we could feed all these people, Philip?" he says, with a knowing gleam in his eye. He might have just winked. "Eat? Are you mad? There's not enough money in Israel, let alone our purses, to cater this party!" he replies. As if on cue, Andrew takes the opportunity to flex his wit. "Here's a boy, Jesus! He's got five loaves and two fish! Think that'll do?!" They all have a laugh at this. Jesus chuckles too. Such a humorous moment. Such a gift. He loves these men. "Tell you what, Philip. Have 'em sit. Right where they are is fine. Go ahead." He does. They do.

And then Jesus begins to word a prayer, the likes of which has never been equaled. Because what comes next is... there's really no other word for it...*miraculous*.

It is quite simply this: everyone eats. Not just an hors d'oeuvre-size portion. Not a smidge, pinch, handful, or cup. They *eat*. Until they're full. Bursting, even. This is lost on us, because we eat so much all the time. But people in the ancient world don't often eat this much at one meal. This is beyond a meal. This is a feast, the amount of food that's reserved for weddings and yearly gatherings.

Jesus does this at a picnic.

But like any picnic, Jesus knows you must clean up after yourself. But the lessons are only just beginning, because he has the twelve pick up the garbage. Twelve basketfuls, in fact. One for each of them. One for each of the tribes. One for each of their understandings that they have just been a part of something that the world had only ever seen one time before.

This is the only miracle that is common to all four gospels. That should give us a hint as to its importance. Indeed, this miracle is loaded with Old Testament freight, because when Jesus does this, he is essentially recreating the provision of manna from Exodus 16. That is the story of the so-called "bread from heaven" that came from beyond the skies at God's behest in order to give his people sustenance. This would not have been lost on the Jews eating bread and fish at Jesus' picnic. In fact, "After the people saw the sign Jesus performed, they began to say, 'Surely this is the Prophet [of Deuteronomy 18:15] who is to come into the world.'" Jesus feeds them, yes, but in so doing, he also makes the boldest of bold statements. The crowds find him again later in the chapter, where we find this exchange:

> [The people say] "Our ancestors ate the manna in the wilderness; as it is written: 'He gave them bread from heaven to eat.'" Jesus said to them, "Very truly I tell you, it is not Moses who has given you the bread from heaven, but it is my Father who gives you the true bread from heaven. For the bread of God is the bread that comes down from heaven and gives life to the world." "Sir," they said, "always give us this bread." Then Jesus declared, "I am the bread of life. Whoever comes to me will never go hungry, and whoever believes in me will never be thirsty."
>
> John 6:31-34

I am the Bread of Life. It's the classic metaphor. And for good reason. It's 30,000 years old. It's instantly recognizable, and universally understood. But something happens with bread that is more than grains and yeast and thermal death points. It is life-giving. It is transformational.

And this is not lost on Jesus. He knows. That's why he says it. *I am the bread of life.* "Your ancestors ate the manna in the wilderness, yet they died," (John 6:49). There is a bread you may eat, one hundred and forty eight of them, in fact, but after eating any of them you will hunger again in a matter of hours.

"But here is the bread that comes down from heaven, which anyone may eat and not die," (John 6:50). Then there is a bread you may eat, after which you will never hunger again.

"I am the living bread that came down from heaven. Whoever eats this bread will live forever. This bread is my flesh, which I will give for the life of the world," (John 6:51). Because it is me. I am the Bread of Life. And I will get inside you, dear clay, and I will cause all sorts of transformations. I will eat your soul bacteria and replace it with the air of the Spirit. I will develop your character and personality as I apply heat and a change your time. Because though you be dead, I will vivify. I will cause you to rise. I give life of a different sort, and that life, your true life, will become a pleasing aroma to the Father.

So here's your homework: go gather some friends, go gather some bread-making ingredients, and make some bread together. Then eat it. Together. You will tell the story of that night for years to come

20 MARK

(Note: before you read this, ask yourself if there's a difference between True and Truth.)

I am standing in a fireplace in Smithville, New Jersey. It is one of those fireplaces that has to be big because its job is to heat a room. Only this is summer, and there is no fire in the fireplace. But this is, in fact, the fireplace in the grand lobby of the historic Smithville Hotel, where George Washington once sat with his colonels and talked battle strategy.

Smithville is one of those historic towns, where the buildings are circa 1760 and shopkeepers wear period costumes: the Colonial version of Gatlinburg.

My parents in-law are taking us on a day trip that includes Smithville. We've just come from Ocean City, NJ, and my son's first ever experience with the sea. It was cold. He cried. Then we got ice cream on the boardwalk.

We walk in and out of the shops. I hustle us out of the hand-made soap store as quickly as possible on the grounds that it is way too girly for my son (read: "me."). And The Boy is just a few months old now, and he is getting hungry, so my wife steps out to a bench in the quad and begins to nurse him. I take this as my opportunity to go exploring.

I head to the Scottish Wear store, because my name is Campbell, and such a store interests me. I might need a kilt. On my way, I can't help noticing the idyllic summer scene before me. I pass a teenage girl in the shade engrossed in a novel about vampires, definitely in her own world. And there is a couple holding hands and eating ice cream, the kind that's swirled high in a cup. They are overweight.

Over by the gazebo there is a photographer with a woman in white and a man in a tux and seven other ladies wearing red. It isn't an actual wedding, just the couple and the wedding party taking the pictures. The bride is stunning, and the groom isn't too shabby, but what strikes me is that the groomsmen aren't there taking pictures, only the bridesmaids. As I ponder this, a ten-year old boy rockets past me with another boy about the same age chasing him as fast as he can. Other kids chase too. But still other kids in the group are frozen. The chasing boy catches the one he is chasing, and after he gets tagged, he freezes. I smile as I remember playing freeze tag in my own childhood.

I walk on. I happen to have a bible. I ponder the upcoming school year. Lessons. My classroom. A speech I must give.

I trip.

On a tree root, which is connected to a tree. Upon which is nailed a sign. Ancient wood, with rough-hewn edges and hand-carved letters which aren't even in English, Colonial-era or otherwise. I look at it, intrigued. "Ιχθυς" it reads, hinting at something exotic. Below it is an arrow.

Icthus, I remember, is the ancient Greek word for "fish," the symbol of which would eventually become the symbol for Christianity. I admit my curiosity is peaked.

I follow the arrow until I come to another sign of the same fashion with another arrow. And this time I can see where the arrow points: to a small, unassuming storefront. It is tiny by comparison, sandwiched in between Ye Olde Candy Shoppe and the Haberdashery. As I approach the door, I notice that it is no ordinary door. It must have taken someone a very, very long time to carve all the intricate detail, sand it, finish it, fit it in the jamb. It is as inspiring as a door could possibly be. But if the front door is intricate, it is nothing compared what I find inside.

The door moans and creaks as I enter. I smell mahogany and varnish and history. The shop is spare, but immaculately kept and essentially decorated. Items in frames look hundreds of years old, or older. The slats of the floor are polished to a high gloss. Handles are twisted, swirled black iron, wrought by someone with a large hammer and an imagination.

The merchandise spreads out before me like a blanket. Even the fixtures echo the intricacy of the door; each is precisely-sized to fit a vast array of writing products. Envelopes. Cards. Rough cotton paper, with bits of flowers pressed into them. Parchment. Vellum. Dozens of pens and quills, the kind you dip in ink wells, in every shape, size, and weight. And ink by the phial in a hundred colors with hand-drawn labels. I touch the parchment. It feels smooth and cold to my fingers. I pick up a pen and nib. It beckons me to write in exaggerated letters with large loops.

"May I help you?" rumbles a voice behind me, a voice like the sound of gravel in August. His words are helpful, but his tone is not. I turn. His eyes pierce me. He is a thousand years old, hunched over an olive wood cane. His face has lines like creek beds, his beard white and crispy.

"I'm just browsing. This is a lovely—"

"Where are you from?" he interrupts. I am thrown for the briefest of pauses.

"Memphis. Texas before that."

"Never heard of it."

"Oh?"

"What's that?" he rumbles, and cocks his head toward my bible.

"This? This is just my bi—"

"I know what it is. It's not *just* anything. I want to know what it's covered with."

"Leather."

"Leather? Hmm."

"Yep."

"You read the sign."

"I did."

Silence hangs. A clock ticks somewhere. The overweight couple passes by the window. They don't come in.

"You look like something's on your mind," he solicits.

"I do?"

"People who carry bibles got something on their mind."

He is as insightful and keen as a razor.

"I was just thinking about this, uh…this speech. I'm supposed to give."

"What is it you do?" he rasps.

"I teach. Junior high kids. Teach them bible at the school back in Memphis."

"Why?"

The question halts me. *"Why?" Did he seriously just ask me that? Well, obviously, it's…*

"Because I believe that it's God's Word, and I want to help them with the answers to life. And beyond." There. A solid answer. I am self-satisfied, and the tiniest bit smug. But his eyes are piercing me again.

"You can't tell them the answers."

"Beg your pardon?"

"You haven't even told them the questions yet. Questions teach far better than answers."

Ok.

More silence.

Slowly he turns and starts walking toward the back of the store. His cane punches the floor like poetry, a Colonial-era Captain Ahab.

"Well? You coming?" he thunders in excitement, still walking away. I put down the pen and nib and scoot after him. We approach the thick, iron door at the back of the store. It is the door version of the shop's hardware: artistically twisted iron bedecking a dungeonous door. It could be from the catacombs under the Roman Coliseum. He grasps the levered handle with a weathered hand and gives it a mighty turn. It clanks open, echoing like a cannon through the shop.

"Where are we going?"

"Good question."

I gulp. I half-expect him to light a torch from a sconce. Behind the door, we are met with more wrought iron: an narrow spiral staircase that is steep and beautiful and tapered, like a dagger a giantess might wield. He leads me downstairs, through a dozen twists of the stairs. I am slightly winded and apprehensive. He is neither.

We finally reach the bottom. I hear a click. A single clear light bulb with a metal chain glows, illuminating a stone floor and walls. Before me is a cavernous space of ancient books, parchments, artifacts, historical accouterments.

"Underground railroad?" I offer, trying to sound like I'm putting historical pieces together.

"Something like that," he returns, cryptically. He surveys the landscape before him as if consulting the card catalogue in his mind. "This way," he rasps, and he stalks toward one of a dozen bookshelves. This shelf has "Ἰχθυς" written where call numbers should be.

He leads me deep into the stacks of dusty volumes and corroded bindings. It gets more dank and mustier by the step: a librarian's hell. He stops abruptly at a particular shelf, scans the volumes. "There," he points upward. The book to which he's pointing is too high for him to reach. I am tall. I reach up for it. It is too thick to hold with one hand. It is surrounded by thick black leather. It is covered with the dust of a thousand stories. I blow it off to reveal a simple Christian fish emblem.

"Open it," he rumbles, his voice close to my ears. I creak open the spine, and its pages crackle before me like a burning bush. My Greek is rusty, but I can make out some of it... Ἀρχὴ τοῦ εὐαγγελίου Ἰησου Χριστοῦ, υἱοῦ τοῦ Θεοῦ....
The beginning of the gospel of Jesus Christ the son of God...

"Is this...is this Mark's Gospel?"

"Yes."

"This looks thousands of years old. Is it authentic?"

"Yes."

I try to take in the enormity of what my sweaty hands are holding. If it is indeed authentic, it is worth millions, not to mention the contribution it would make to critical study of the New Testament. But somehow none of that is the most important thing at the moment.

"Where did you get this?"

His eyes pierce me again. The smallest of grins curls across his lips.

"I wrote it."

"What do you mean, 'you wrote it.' Are you saying, you're…"

"Mark."

"As in…"

"The author. Yes."

No. It couldn't be. I am now frightened. This could be a delusion. No one knows where I am. I have no cell phone signal. No one can hear me now. Or it could be real. Or it could be a con. Any moment I expect to awaken in a bathtub full of ice with my kidneys missing.

"Scared doesn't answer questions, son. Calm down. Let me show you something. Look." And like a man holding his newborn, he flips the pages. "Can you read this?" he rasps.

"I can try…"

"Look at the first chapter. Notice anything?"

I scan it. "You used 'immediately' and 'at once' quite a bit."

"Ever wonder why?"

"I always assumed you were writing quickly; that you wanted to get it all down before you forgot." Again with the piercing eyes. "Youth and their assumptions."

"Hang on. Does this mean…are you telling me…you actually walked…with *him*?"

"Not long. But yes."

"What was he like."

"You have read the book, yes?"

"Yeah, but I mean really. What was it like to be around him?"

"Your questions are getting better." His eyes are as alive as they have ever been.

"It was a constant examination. Of the world. Of God. Of self. He never quit helping you to see things differently. And then you'd start to get the feeling that *he* was normal and *we* were the ones who had it all wrong. Keep reading. Verse twenty-five and following. Jesus heals a person by casting out a demon, and in the next few verses he's famous throughout the region. People are asking questions like, 'What is this? A new teaching?' But the questions don't stop there."

He gingerly flips the page. "Chapter two verse six. Pharisees are questioning Jesus in their own hearts." Flip. "Chapter four verse thirty-five. Jesus calms the storm, and the disciples are so struck they ask 'Who is this that even the wind and the sea obey him?' This was one of the questions they were always asking."

Another flip of the page. "Chapter six verse thirty. He gathers everyone together out in the middle of nowhere. It is late in the day, people are getting edgy. And he tells the twelve to feed them all—all five thousand men, as many women and not a few children. Well, Andrew, the smart brother, grabs this young kid who's holding a couple of fish and the next thing they know, Jesus is recreating God feeding Israel in the desert. It's the only miracle all four of us wrote in common. And it wasn't lost on the crowd, either. They got it. They started to whisper and point, and that was Jesus' cue to leave. But look down at verse forty-five: he backed up what he'd just done by walking on water. He called Peter of all people out of the boat, and the people really started to talk. They were asking all sorts of questions."

"But they still didn't totally get it, which is why," he flips the page, "I put in the story of the half-healed blind man."

I am putting the pieces together. "It's a metaphor."

"Yes. Of what it means to see Jesus clearly. You can imagine what people were saying about him!"

I looked up at the old man who looks fifty years younger as he tells me all this. "I'm sure they were thinking 'Who is this guy?'"

"Indeed," he returned, as he ever so gently turned the page. "Look at chapter eight verse twenty-two through thirty. It is the fulcrum of the book, because I wrote chapters one through eight to make the reader ask 'Who is this man Jesus?' Jesus even poses the question to Peter: 'Who do you say that I am?' And Peter, who was much sharper than we give him credit for, says back, 'You're the Christ.' And the question is answered."

I stand in silence for several moments reading the ancient scrawl.

"That's incredible."

"Thank you."

"There's more, isn't there?"

"There's always more."

"Tell me about chapters nine through sixteen. Because you said you wrote one through eight to answer 'Who is Jesus?' What question did you write nine through sixteen to answer?"

"A fine question. Very fine." He grins the grin of a schoolmaster whose lessons are starting to seep through. He gingerly flips the page.

"Look here at chapter nine, verses eighteen through thirty-three. The disciples are at a loss in discussing their failure to drive out demons. But Jesus doesn't question their methods; he questions their faith when he elaborates upon that which is possible to him to believes. Then he finishes with a discussion of who is the greatest. 'If you want to be first, be last. If you want to lead, be a servant.' Those were hard words, even for him."

"So the question is 'Who is the greatest?'"

"Not quite. Look further. Chapter ten: Jesus challenges Pharisees, adults, wealthy, but in verse twenty-nine, he sweetens the deal. 'Yes, following me will incur sacrifices, but the payoff is far greater than you can imagine, even in this life now.'"

"Because people weren't sure they wanted to follow him, even after the events in chapters one through eight?"

"Oh, they wanted to follow him. He was never wanting for followers, not until the end. But Jesus wanted to make sure they were serious. The only way to do that is to hold up a mirror."

"You had mirrors?"

"It's a figure of speech."

"Ah."

He flips the page, gentle as a butterfly. "Look at chapter ten verse thirty-two. There were many for whom the mirror was sour, and those who followed were afraid! Even so...they followed."

"What kind of person follows even though they're afraid?" I said, more to myself than him.

"That's your best question yet."

"Well, what's the answer?"

He smirks and reads on. "They watch him heal a blind man, completely this time—what does that say? They watch him curse a fig tree. They watch him wreck havoc in the temple. They watch him tangle with experts in the Law. One of them asks him, 'Which commandment is the greatest?'"

"Not a good question."

"I don't think so either. But Jesus actually answered him, even quoting Law back to him. Love the Lord with all you have, and love each other too. Anyone, *anyone* who reads that is forced into the mirror and ask 'Can I do this?' And this teacher of the Law, he got it. He got that fully dedicating oneself to God and loving each other hour in and hour out, day in and day out was far more important than all the temple offerings and sacrifices."

"I just taught that several months ago! Samuel knew it. Amos knew it. Hosea knew it. They all knew it. Obedience is greater than sacrifice."[66]

"Which is why Jesus praised the man in the next few verses when he told him he is not far from the kingdom. To a people looking for a messiah, that would have washed over them like the morning tide on New Year's Day."

"It's still a tall order, though: love God hour to hour and love people Monday through Saturday, not just Sunday."

"Indeed."

"*I* struggle with that. Can't imagine how they felt, hearing it fresh."

"Afraid."

"I'm sure they were."

"Me, too."

He flips the page one last time. "I ended my book at chapter sixteen verse eight, but God saw fit to end it further on. I didn't argue. But look at that verse."

"You ended it with people fleeing the empty tomb terrified."

"Do you see?"

"See what?"

"Do you *see?*"

I look again at the text. And I see it. They were scared. Afraid.

"Terrified."

But we have the book. So they must have passed on the story in spite of their fear. They must have summoned a courage greater than their own in order to become part of a larger epic, yet play an integral role in it. I wonder if I could have done that. I wonder if I *would* have done that. *Who am I?*

"Who am *I?*"

That's it. That's what chapters nine through sixteen of Mark were written to make the readers ask! Who is Jesus? Who am I? That's it! I am excited at this nugget mined from the depths. I turn. Mark is already spiraling halfway up the spiral staircase. He is positively spritely.

We reach the ornate iron door. I wonder out loud if I would have had the courage to face the kind of antagonism the early Christians faced if it meant that the story would not be passed on if I failed. "I wonder what kind of believer I really am."

"Let me show you something else," he beckons in a gravely baritone. We proceed back through the door, to the front of the shop.

"What do you see?"

"People."

"What kind of people?"

"I don't know. *People.* People doing things."

"They're the answers."

"I'm sorry?"

"Over there. A girl. Reading a book about vampires. She's a picture. Because there are Vampire Christians out there. They want Jesus for his blood and nothing else. They are only interested in the forgiveness, not the new life that comes with it."[67]

He shifts his eyes. "And over there. The bridesmaids. What do you see?"

"Bridesmaids."

"There are Bridesmaids Christians out there. They look like they're the bride of Christ. They're beautiful and they stand at the altar next to the groom. But they don't take the vows. They don't say 'I do.' They are not the bride."[68]

He shuffles to the other window, points with his olive-wood cane. "Over that way. The kids in the yard. What are they doing?"

"Running."

"What else?"

"Playing. A game. Tag. Freeze tag."

"There are Christians who play that game: Freeze Tag Christians. They get touched by the master, but then they freeze. They don't tell the story. They just keep showing up Sunday after Sunday, expecting to be fed. They are the frozen chosen. They consume church. It does not consume them."

"And there. The couple with the ice cream."

"Walking?"

"There are Christians who are Soft Serve Christians. Totally in love with Jesus, but spiritually overweight. They are interested in the sweet, but they eschew the sweat. They enjoy the lovely, the introspective, the meaningful song, the worship atmosphere. They don't feed homeless, or visit shut-ins, or paint houses for elderly. Reflection was meant to be descriptive, not proscriptive. Service is what feeds the soul, not reflection. If solitary bible reading and reflection is boring, it is because there is nothing new in the soul to consider."

I turn my gaze. I see my wife and son. He sees them too. I desperately try to anticipate what he'll say next. My phone tinks. The text message says, "Where are you?" *Where indeed? Good question.*

"It's good for your boy to have milk now. It keeps him alive and grows him strong. But one day he'll need solid food. See that he gets it."

"Literally or metaphorically?"

"Yes."

Silence hangs. The clock still ticks.

"How am I supposed to tell all this to junior high students in my speech?"

He turns to me. His eyes beam.

"That's a good question."

21   LIGHT & DARK

We are near the end. So let us return to the beginning. There's a verb there you've probably missed all these years, as I did.

In the epic poem that is the creation story of Genesis 1, God comes into close proximity to an entity which is formless and empty. This is how the world is described in Genesis 1:2. And as it happens, such a description serves as more or less the poetic outline for the chapter. On day one, He creates the light. But then—and here's the verb—he *separates* the light from the darkness. On day two, he creates the waters above and the waters below. Then he *separates* the waters above from the waters below and puts a big space in between them called "sky." The implication is that there used to be an eighth layer to our atmosphere: a sphere of water between us and orbit.

On day three, he calls the dry ground to emerge from the seas. The word "separate" is not used on day three, but the implication is there. And in these three days, what has he done but bring order to the chaos. What has he done but bring form to that which was formless. He has created—and separated— the three elemental orders or our terrestrial existence: air, sea and land. It is Him and His Presence bursting onto the scene that gives the light. Because light is where he is. And he is here.

By the time day four commences, he is done with the form. Now he's on to the filling. And what does he fill on day four but the sun, the moon, and stars to govern the day and the night, to make a distinction between light and darkness.[69] On day five, he fills the sky with winged creatures of every sort, and he populates the sea with the flora and fauna of the ocean. On day six he sets out to infuse the land with life. So he creates land life. And of all the creatures of the land, the apex, pinnacle, and zenith was none other than man himself. Male and female they are created, in his very own image.

The earth is no longer formless and empty. It has shape, an infrastructure, a context. And that space is filled with all life as we know it from eagles to algae, hydrangeas to hippos. And every bit of it is declared "good."

And the crowning jewel is us. Because in us God makes a distinction: we are made in his image. And we are the only thing made in his image, according to Genesis 1. It is by making this distinction that God separates us. And when he sees us in our place among the totality of creation, he declares it "very good." He thinks very highly of us.

But he's just getting started. What he does next is even more incredible: he stops. I know it says "rests" in most English bibles, and that's unfortunate because that word casts the idea that God is tuckered out and needs to grab a cup of coffee to make it through the afternoon. That is simply not true. That's not anywhere near the zip code of true. That's not even an accurate generalization. A better rendering is that he simply "ceases." He stops. He puts the brakes on, holds up, pauses the action. But pay close attention: he still creates, even on day seven.

In days 1-6, he's just finished making all kinds of distinctions in space. Now on day 7, he makes a distinction in time. He separates it from the rest of the days. He creates it *by not creating*.

He's that creative. I've never created anything by not creating. Everything I create I have to create. Even then, it's mostly just reordering stuff that's already there. I don't create the raw materials. But he did. And then he stopped. And still created. And still separated. And still made a distinction.

This Sabbath day is fundamentally different than the other days: it is not declared "good," or even "very good." It is declared "holy." God is Holy principally because he is distinct and other.[70] This is the essential message of all the Prophets. With this word, holy, God forges into a new realm of the reality of creation. There is now an aspect of creation that has some of God's very own character and ethos. There is none like God, and there is no day like this day.

Now there is a holiness that belongs to God which we will never be able to achieve, because he is infinitely other, infinitely beyond and distinct. But there is a holiness we can achieve, and he gives us a way to do it: make distinctions between light and darkness, just as he did in Genesis 1. Now as then, he longs to speak light into the formless chaos of our lives, fill them with that which is good, and make us distinct. We can choose to act like him. Indeed, the battle cry of Leviticus is "be holy because I am holy."[71] We can make distinctions between that which is good, lovely, kind, winsome, true, beautiful, noble, and that which is deceitful, arrogant, prideful, cunning, inappropriate, crass, hateful, dark, and soul-sucking.

This is why he put the Tree of the Knowledge of Good and Evil in the Garden in the first place. He could have left it out and removed all possibility of sin. Instead, he put it in. The cynic's answer is that God is testing us. "You have a choice, Adam. Follow my instructions not to eat of that tree, or ignore my instructions and eat it." And this is why Commandment #4 ("Remember the Sabbath, keep it holy") would become such a revered part of the Israelite existence. It was a way to be like God, to connect the image of God within you to him. It was virtually a commandment to go visit a Thin Place on every seventh day.[72]

I prefer the glass-half-full approach in explaining why he put the tree in the Garden: he imbues us with distinction-making capacity, trusts us to do just that, and then gives us opportunity to prove ourselves. He says, in essence, "Adam, choose to live out the part of yourself that is like me, or choose to live out of the part of yourself that is not like me. You can do it. I believe in you." When Adam was formed, and when you were formed, and when I was formed, he and we were made in God's image. There is part of him in us. And to the point of holiness, humanity is the *only* thing made in God's image, and is therefore distinct, bearing a bit of holiness too. Because everything God created down here is of the physical dimension, and everything that is in the spiritual dimension is, well, spirit. But there is a nexus, a connection, a Thin Place in perpetuity between these two worlds.

It is you.

Because you are physical, yet you have a spiritual component: God's very breath within you.[73] Rob Bell makes the point that we humans are the one thing in creation that are both body and spirit. Or perhaps, even that is backwards. As George MacDonald said, perhaps "you don't have a soul. Perhaps you are a soul, and you have a body."[74]

But here is where Bell and MacDonald and all the rest fall short: they only make a case for our *knowing* that we are spiritual. But just knowing that we are spiritual is not enough, because that doesn't reveal any distinction-making action on our part. What should be done with this reality and what does it reveal about God, and us? What must we do, in light of the spirit within? The answer pertains to us now and then.

22 NOW & THEN

What if you existed outside of time?

I know, I know. It's nuts. Just go with me.

Suppose it's 11:33pm, and you're sitting in a chair, the chair in your living room, perhaps. What if you could snap your fingers and stop time? The clock would stay at 11:33. What if you got up and went walking across the room and stood by the shelf? *Now* you would be in the chair and by the shelf at 11:33. You would be in two places at the same *time*. Because it's still *now*.

The movie *Interstellar* got me thinking about this. I loved the film, but I knew Matthew McConaughey was in trouble as soon as they traveled through a worm hole out by Saturn to get to the water planet. Then they took longer exploring the water planet than anticipated and complications arose. He looked up at the mountains and dread crossed his face, and he said, "Those aren't mountains." And sure enough, they weren't. They were tsunamis. And they were headed his way. They fired up the ship, blew the water out of the engines, and blasted off just in the nick of time, so to speak.

But when they get back to the space station in orbit, their compatriot Romily who stayed behind, is now twenty-three years older, and he's been there by himself for all that time.

When Captain McConaughey went down to the water planet, there was a time dilation because of its proximity to at the black hole Gargantua. An hour on the planet equals seven years of Earth time. They're down there for three and half hours. Chaos ensues.

See, a worm hole is (very) basically like this: imagine the universe as a sheet of notebook paper. There's an X up by the top blue line, and a Y down by the bottom edge. Now if you want to travel through the space from X to Y, you have to draw a line and travel the distance of the paper, about nine inches, let's say, i.e., millions of light years in space terms. But if you took the paper and bent it back over on itself, to where X and Y were almost touching, then to travel from X to Y you would only have to go an inch or so. That's a worm hole. I won't spoil the movie for you, but suffice to say, it'll have you thinking about time very differently.

Yes, I know wormholes only exist in theory. Stay with me.

What if there's a worm hole from Creation to Revelation? To get from beginning to end though history, you have to begin at The Beginning of the map, cross the Mountain Pass of Exodus, the Plains of Samuel and Kings, the Oasis of Psalms, the Outpost of the Prophets, the four hundred years of biblical desert between the testaments, the Highlands of Jesus, Valley of his Death, the Mountain of the Resurrection, the Sea of the Spirit, the urban sprawl of the Church, and finally, the Rift Canyon of Revelation.

But what if you could bend the biblical history back on itself so that Revelation and Genesis were just a few acres apart? What if they're not separated by distance, but by time? They are, after all, a book of Beginnings and a book of New Beginnings. Sin, as it tends to do, complicates things. Shalom, order, and peace are disrupted, and God no longer resided here, so he goes there. Ah, but one day, *then*, something new will happen. But it won't happen there. It will happen here.

In Creation, which happens over seven days in the context of Genesis,[75] there is distinction made in the very first verse about God creating two separate entities: heavens and earth. God is still very much in both places. But what if they are not separated in the way we've assumed all these years: by *only* space. In Revelation, we do not leave here and go there. In the New Creation, there will come here. Once again, the two will be one. The distinction will be erased as New Heaven and New Earth are fused together. But notice: it's not a distinction in place that will be erased. It's a distinction in *time*. *New* is a term relative to time, not space. And Jesus didn't say, "I am coming *there*." He said, "I am coming *soon*." What if Jesus is the passage, path, and the portal—the worm hole—though which all of Creation touches ReCreation?

So when does that start? When does the *then* start becoming *now*? There's a clue in 2 Corinthians 1:22 which tells us the Holy Spirit is a "guaranteed deposit." It comes down here now to rest on the newly faithful life of a believer, and offers its regenerative powers to our souls. We don't get it all now, but we get a small taste.

God separates not just space, but time when he puts part of his Spirit here, inside us, and part of his Spirit remains there with him. It's like the part Spirit that lives in the believer now is the embassy in a foreign country; it's sovereign territory of the home country, except that it's far away. And one day God is going to reunite the Holy Spirit that is here with the Holy Spirit that is there. But remember, God is outside of time, so he's going to reunite the now with the then, in the same place, here. When Jesus returns and all is made right, regenerative power is the kind of thing that will happen *then*. But it also happens on a much smaller scale, *here now*.

I realize this discussion wades into some pretty deep existential water, but it's important for precisely this reason: Life is not about fixing the sin problem. Life is not a test. It's not a trek though history. It is those things, but it is not *about* those things; they are consequences and collateral affairs in the process of what life IS about.

Life is about taking our place as God's image bearers to restore shalom to the earth, in preparation for the future day when Heaven will come down to Earth and there will no longer be *here* and *there*. It's not a *here* or *there* issue. It's a *now* and *then* issue.[76] We are here to make now look like then.

When you lie down in the stillness and quiet night, do you find yourself with a profound sadness you can neither explain nor assuage, or with a hope rumbling deep beneath your soul like the purr of the sea? Do you lament your choices, or rejoice over them? When the curve balls come, and they will, do you somehow feel guilty because you didn't hit them? Or do you face them with confidence and swing away? When you see the thing for which your heart desperately longs, does it fill with you joy…or despair? When you say goodbye to what you must, do you weep in the farewell, or in the reunion you know you must have one day?

If you're human, chances are these are not either/or questions. They are yes questions, because they are the now longing for the then. Somewhere inside of us, we know we are living in the tension between the now and the then, the already and the not yet.

But there are dangers. If you make your life all about the *now*, you will suffer unending ache. If you make your life all about the *then*, you will go mad at limitless potential unreached. Our lives must touch both, because with each passing hour on the universe's clock, eternities are being born that will be here soon.

I know it's tough. Believe me, I know. Please. Please, hold on. Just a little longer. I'm asking you. Just hold on. You can do this. Then is coming. He who testifies to these things says, "Surely I am coming soon." Amen. Come, Lord Jesus! The grace of the Lord Jesus be with all. Amen.[77]

23 MIST

If the first point of contact between God's realm and this one was humans, the second was the tabernacle: the holy, yet mobile tent where His presence was dwelling with His people. Some years later, the tabernacle was replaced by the permanent Temple, a structure made of stone and laid upon a foundation. God's presence dwelt there too when it was completed,[78] and this ushered in a new era of how God's Spirit was present among his people.

Several dozen more generations went by, and Jesus appeared on the scene. Not just God's Spirit this time, but God Himself in fleshly form; this is the beauty and scandal of the incarnation. But God doesn't stop there. Once Jesus resurrects and goes back to the Father, he sends the Holy Spirit to dwell on earth once again. Only this time, it's not in a literal tent or a building, but a metaphorical one: your body.

This is the hallmark of the Christian, our stamp, badge, imprint, and calling card. God's Spirit in us. And right there is where our battle lines are drawn every single minute of every single hour of every single day of our entire lives. That is the choice that hits us every day. "Be like God, or be like me." Be beautiful or be hot. Offer my strength to one woman, or get in as many beds as I can. Tell the IRS, or keep the tips to myself.

Be kind, or say something awful and follow it with "I'm just kidding." Be pure in speech, or cuss like a sailor. Play fair, or play dirty. Build up, or gossip. Revere the name, or throw around OMG! Buy them a sandwich, or pretend you don't see them and lock your doors. Study for a C, or cheat for an A. Work hard, or sleep with someone important. Separate light from darkness, or blend them together and spend your life in a sea of gray.

When we, these potential shells for the Spirit, are born, we go from darkness to the light of life. We are a fetus in a dark, inside world and become a fully functioning human being in an outside world. I'm told one of the reasons babies cry so much when they're born is that everything is so bright. When my children were born, it was no different. After all the contractions and breathing, after all the pushing, about ninety seconds was all it took for them to transform from a potentiality to a reality. Of course, their actual lives began months earlier, but being born is a shock, a disruptive, violent step forward in development.

It was very bright, that I remember. The lights were very low and almost moody while my wife was pushing. I was holding her hand. But the doctors knew when the event was imminent, and when the moment of truth arrived, suddenly there were so many blinding lights from every direction I thought Jesus was in the room. And Humphrey entered the world. Several years later, Sam, then Ilsa. Squinting. And crying. I did too. So did you, most likely. Above all, they wanted to be held, warmed, and comforted. I'm not sure they or we will ever stop wanting these things. These things make the violence bearable.

And then some time passes, and there comes a moment when we are touched by God and by Jesus to such a degree that we want to be a part of him, to be adopted. So like Nicodemus stealing away at night, we explore what it means to be "born again," to borrow language from John 3.

We decide to go through with it, our conversion, once again going through a disruption of development, this time in the spiritual realm; a spiritually violent act of war that begins a life of seeking peace and pursuing it. We go from the dark and insulatory life spent in pursuit of self, spiritually kicking and sucking our thumb, to the holy, blinding light of a life spent in pursuit of Other. This new life is Spirit, and it is bright. People can see it. It is a shock to the system at first, this living for someone else, ever serving, ever turning the other cheek, ever dying to self. It is an upside down kingdom to which we are called to be subject. And it is ridiculously difficult. So I cry. So do you, most likely. Cry for comfort. Cry to be held through it. Cry to feel warmth in our souls. Cry to know we're not crazy and our choices really do matter. I'm not sure we'll ever stop wanting these things. They assuage the spiritual violence and assault.

And some more time passes, decades roll past like stripes on the highway. We look back in retrospect, and fill our walls with portraits. We relish every phone call. We set our affairs in order. If we are a person of faith, and we live out all that Jesus intended us to be, we are bursting to see glory's face. We look forward to being with the Lord in a place where there will be no more tears, nor shingles, nor kidney failure, nor detached retinas, nor confusion, nor chemo, nor death. We long to be normal again, how we were *back then*, when we were young and full of color; when our souls were verdant as the springtime and our muscles robust as the stag's. But we can neither escape nor deny the finality.

Whether heroes or cowards, one way or another the rhythm of our breath will rest, and we will sleep. And when we die at the end of this life, yet again we will go from darkness to a far greater light. Our temporal world here was declared *good* in Genesis 1, yet from the perspective of *there, by God's side*...it will be dim by comparison, not because this world here is so fundamentally different than that world there, but because when all things are made new, that world there will enter this world here. We don't *go* to heaven. Heaven comes *here*.

The new heavens and the new earth happen here, according to Revelation, but *here* will be cast in shadowy relief when we stand in the presence of the He Who Is Light, He Who Is Love, He Who Is. It will be a different *here* because it won't be the *here now* but the *here then*. Just as the Sabbath day was distinct from the other six days of creation not in space but in time, so the new heavens and new earth will be distinct in time, but not space.

One of the angels at the tomb after the resurrection asked Mary and Mary Magdalene, "Why do you seek the living among the dead. He is not here, but has risen."[79] The angel's verbiage assumes that Jesus had gone on living even though he died. In some sense, then, being born is dying, and dying is being born. Who we are in the middle affects everything else. Because where these two places meet is a very thin place between two realities. It is in the separating of light and darkness that we discover it again and again and again:

Love.

This world now is not Love's home.[80] Love is not of the realm of the created now. It is of the realm of the Creator then. Love was not made in Genesis 1. Love was the agent and catalyst. It is not from around these parts. When it shows up down here now, it is a foreigner to our land, a tourist taking a trip through the countryside. That's why Love—noble, selfless Love —looks so odd to the passersby. People just don't *act* that way. It's not normal, and we're not used to really, I mean *really* seeing it very often.

Love speaks a different language, and has different customs. It uses different currency than the locals, and its exchange rate is ridiculously high; you might take a beating in the transaction. But we want to be around it. It tells different sorts of stories, dances to different music and embraces different traditions. Yet it is somehow welcome here now. Because Love walks further, gives more, complains less. It teaches, inspires, radiates and promises. It changes us, moves us, grows us. It invites us to know and be known and loved anyway, because in this, Love gives us a glimpse beyond and a glimpse of that day when the future becomes the now.

Why? Because a day is coming when there will be no more thin places. Because there will be no more veil. There will become here. Then will become now.

We don't yet see things clearly. We're squinting in a fog, peering through a mist. But it won't be long before the weather clears and the sun shines bright! We'll see it all then, see it all as clearly as God sees us, knowing him directly just as he knows us!

1 Cor. 13:12 (MSG)

Maybe Jesus has been in the room the whole time.

EPILOGUE: SWIM

If you've stuck with me this long, I thank you. Hopefully you have realized some thin places that have appeared in your own life, perhaps in retrospect. If not...will you take a trip with me?

That night at the Waffle House in Arkansas felt so...paternal. Like something a dad would teach: Love is not accurately measured by how favored a person is. At the Waffle House, I had discovered a thin place when I discovered an aspect of reality wherein I have nothing to do with how favored I am. Just because you might have a bunch of stuff, or ability, or cash doesn't mean God loves you more. This can be confusing because we have a tendency to think God loves us the way we love him, but that is utter nonsense.

All parents, God included, love their children immeasurably more than children love their parents. That's just how it is. And they want their kids to know how much they love them, but they also want the kids to figure some of that out on their own. So the parents drop just enough clues in the right spots and at the right times so that the child will come to his own correct conclusion. When God does this, I believe the clues are the thin places. And the living of life, in many ways, is in the noticing. Because on some very seldom occasions, when I stop and breathe and see with my soul, the noticing reveals to me that my world is perceptively close to God's world. I hope the same for you.

The next time you're at the beach, make a point to stand at the edge of the water and look out as far as you can see. Let the surf wash over your ankles. To be so small, staring out into something so big. And then to realize you are on a tiny planet at the edge of something that takes light years to get across. It would be like standing on one kind of beach, while standing on another kind of beach. And the water would be blue or green, depending what ocean you're looking at, and it would remind you of the color of the background of your dreams.

The trouble is, the tide would eventually come in. And if you were still standing there, you'd be waist deep in water without ever having moved, sand ever shifting beneath your feet and not a thing to grab onto. And something huge several million miles away caused all this madness. This is itself not a bad metaphor for how life will turn on you. There you are going about your business, driving the same beautiful route you always drive, and then you get t-boned by a drunk ambassador with government plates and diplomatic immunity, so you can do exactly nothing.

Stay in one place too long—spiritually or physically— and the sand beneath you will eventually shift, usually about the time a breaker is coming at you. You will be thrown off balance and you will fall. And the undertow may be subtle at first, but it will pull you down into the extreme, or worse, into apathy. Oh, it will still be beautiful to look at, the sea, but by then you will know it also can be treacherous, even deadly.[81]

Don't leave the coast yet. You have one more stop to make: go take in a view of the ocean while standing on the jetty, those large outcroppings of man-laid stone at the edge of the ship channel. They are stalwart breakwaters, sentries standing post to defend the harbor when the storms come. The ocean itself doesn't look all that different when you're on such a massive rock pile, but what your standing on makes all the difference in the world. Because the moon will still wax and wane, and the same tide will come in at the same time. But when you're standing on the jetty, the rock, your footing is sure. These boulders are not affected by the tide.

And if you'll look closely at the jetty, you might happen upon a little pool, a pool created by a tide long ago.[82] There it is, just down the way. A lovely pool, no bigger than a coffee table. And there's algae around the edge of the thing, the lime green kind that looks as though it's radioactive. But look closer.

There is a whole little world in there. The tiniest of creatures, all living in perfect harmony and, as evidenced by the algae, having done so for quite sometime. Mr. Crab and Mr. Starfish wave at each other with the morning paper under their arms. Miss Minnow is swimming laps. Mrs. Squid sips her coffee as she takes the kids to soccer practice. Mr. Limpet mows his tiny yard with his riding mower.

But the waxing is coming. Soon the tide will be in. And when it does, the water of the ocean will spill into the pool. This perfect little self-contained world, which thinks it's all on its own because it has no memory of its creation, will be introduced and connected to a far bigger world. Every handful of hours it will come into contact with a better world, a bluer world, the depths and wonders of which it could not possibly imagine.

Of course there is danger out there in the bigger world. Of course there are sharks, and of course the reefs can be treacherous. But the glory will be staggering. Because lest we forget, this ocean teeming with life—all kinds of life—was declared *good* at creation. And it has only improved since.

Every now and again, your tide will come in. You will look with your soul, as you discover a thin place. You and your world will be exposed to a bigger and better world, a more amazing world, a brighter and more staggering world, the depths and wonders of which you cannot possibly imagine. Miss it, and you miss that which has been prepared for you. Because no matter how comfortable you are, the fact remains that you were not made for life in the tiny pool. You were made for the grander ocean.

When that moment comes, when the tide comes in, swim.

Duncan Campbell has been in student ministry for two decades and is passionate about creating a space to make the bible come alive to young people. He currently serves as the student life minister at the New Braunfels Church of Christ in New Braunfels, Texas. He earned his Masters in Bible (Old Testament) from the Harding School of Theology in Memphis, Tennessee. He and his wife have three children.

Acknowledgements

Thank you to all the students, past and present, whom I've ever had the honor of teaching. Your enthusiasm is contagious. Teaching your hearts has taught mine.

Thank you to my church family, past and present, who entrust me with the care and keeping of the spirits of the young. I love you all.

Thank you to my parents, John and Patricia, and my late father Doug, who gave me lots of love, pens, and stories.

Thank you to my dear children. You are my treasures who show me the Maker every single day. I'm absolutely nuts about you three and so grateful to be your dad.

Thank you to my dear and beautiful wife Sherah for sharing this journey with me. Thank you for cheering me on when I dream big dreams.

Notes

[1] William Stafford, *The Way It Is* (Minneapolis: Graywolf Press, 1998).

[2] Bell, Rob. "There's a Bit More Going on Here" (MP3 sermon recording). Sermon, Mars Hill Church, Grandville, MI, 2006.

[3] In fact, I was going to write a whole chapter on how the elements of story mimic and echo the elements of living our lives, but Donald Miller beat me to it. If you've not read his *A Million Miles In A Thousand Years*, you should.

[4] Indeed, buckets of ink have been spilled writing on this very topic; I won't belabor the point here.

[5] Exodus 36:2ff

[6] "For a thousand years in your sight
   are but as yesterday when it is past,
   or as a watch in the night."

[7] Although my reference to this information was from a live performance of Louie Giglio and Chris Tomlin on the Indescribable Tour, Giglio later wrote a book on the subject containing a more substantial treatment. Giglio, Louie, and Matt Redman. *Indescribable: Encountering the Glory of God in the Beauty of the Universe* (Colorado Springs: David C. Cook, 2011).

[8] Psalm 19:1

[9] It's worth noting that of all the characters in the Bible who talk about Hell, Jesus talks about it the most.

[10] http://www.mindbodygreen.com/0-1102/Joan-Rivers-on-Love-Fear-and-Passion-for-Your-Work.html

[11] Come to think of it, the Burt Lancaster character is a lot like Jesus in that respect.

[12] In John 7:37, he essentially tells the crowd, "Believe in me first. Then I'll reveal to you who I am." This is 180° opposite of the 'Seeing-is-Believing" cliché. For Jesus, it's "Believing-is-Seeing."

[13] Ephesians 5:31-33.

[14] Eldredge, John. *Wild at Heart: Discovering the Passionate Soul of a Man* (Nashville: T. Nelson, 2001), 29-32.

[15] Gen. 1:26-27

[16] Psalm 27:4

[17] The ideas presented in this chapter find their genesis in a fuller treatment of the material in question in Joe Beam, *Seeing the Unseen* (Shreveport: Howard,1992), 67-69. I here give Mr. Beam full credit for his ideas distilled here.

[18] Beam, 68.

[19] This paragraph, Beam, 69.

[20] I'm grateful to Billy Wilson, one of my favorite preachers ever, for saying it just this way.

[21] This is a paraphrase of Ross Douthat's "During a frustrating argument with a Roman Catholic cardinal, Napoleon Bonaparte supposedly burst out: "Your eminence, are you not aware that I have the power to destroy the Catholic Church?" The cardinal, the anecdote goes, responded ruefully: "Your majesty, we, the Catholic clergy, have done our best to destroy the church for the last 1,800 years. We have not succeeded, and neither will you." http://www.nytimes.com/2010/03/29/opinion/29douthat.html

[22] Cornelius's story is in Acts 10.

[23] Why, then, must it die once we leave college? Let's start a church camp that really is for the whole church, i.e., all age demographics. That would be awesome.

[24] McKee, Robert. *Story: Style, Structure, Substance, and the Principles of Screenwriting* (New York: HarperCollins, 1997), 5.

[25] Ibid., 414.

[26] Ecclesiastes 3:11

[27] "Paul Revere's Ride," Wikipedia, 31 July 2012.

[28] Ibid.

[29] It should not be missed that Longfellow's famous poem was published in 1861 as a boon to Union sensibilities. It was not seen as an elevation of Revere and his patriots in and of themselves, but as a comparison of those patriots to Longfellow's fellow Union supporters to make the point that history favors the brave.

[30] This is a shoutout to Orwell's *Animal Farm*.

[31] This may have been true during the prophetic era in the Old Testament, but Hebrews 1:1-2 tells us that God spoke via many media but has finally and most completely spoken through his son Jesus. For another prophet (a spirit-filled person truly speaking on God's behalf as in the Old Testament) to come on the scene now would diminish Jesus's nature and character as the last revelation. It would also compromise the truth of Hebrews 1:1-2 with respect to Jesus and render it obsolete.

[32] This, of course, begs the question: Are there Spirituopaths?

[33] Romans 6:1-14

[34] Maxwell, John. *Everyone Communicates, Few Connect* (Nashville: Thomas Nelson, 2010), 205.

[35] This is precisely one of the overarching themes of the book of Ecclesiastes.

[36] cf. Matthew 23:23

[37] I acknowledge that the physical body is part of this equation too, but that's a discussion for another chapter.

[38] Chesterton, G.K., *Orthodoxy* (New York: Doubleday, 1959), 13.

[39] John 5:39-40

[40] There is a discussion among scholars as to whether the Bible is Theocentric, i.e. God-centered, or Christocentric, i.e. Christ-centered. Admittedly, saying that the point of the Scriptures is Jesus, makes it sound as though I advocate a Christo-centric point of view. However, I believe the God-centered/Christ-centered discussion is simply two sides of the same coin. If one believes Jesus was God in the flesh, then it's a moot discussion anyway, as it's based on a false dichotomy. When asked whether the bible is God-centered or Christ-centered, my response is simply, "Yes."

[41] John 2:12-22

[42] Exodus 23:15

[43] Damon Lindleof and Carlton Cuse did the same thing in the middle of the LOST t.v. series, when they started making the flashbacks flash forwards instead, but their idea got a lot more press than the last supper. Still, there's nothing new under the sun.

[44] Cf. Matthew 5:17

[45] E.g., Eph. 2:14-16

[46] Gal. 3:19ff; Rom. 10:4ff;

[47] Isaiah. 49:6

[48] The Hebrew word *hesed* is here translated as "steadfast love." This is a notoriously difficult word to translate. It means something like *loyal, kind, gentle, faithfulness and affection* all wrapped up into one word. Jackie A. Naudè, "הסד," in *The New International Dictionary of Old Testament Theology and Exegesis*, ed. Willem VanGemeren (Grand Rapids: Zondervan, 1997), 2:276-7.

[49] Matt. 7:22-23

[50] Ironically, Ritual is one of the easiest things to elevate to idol.

[51] I capitalize "It" only for the sake of keeping antecedents straight.

[52] Singer/Songwriter David Wilcox wrote a scathing critique of the music industry with his song *Sex & Music* from his album "Underneath," 1999.

[53] Exodus 20:2ff

[54] This is a distillation of Bruce K. Waltke, "Proverbs: Theology of," in *The New International Dictionary of Old Testament Theology and Exegesis*, ed. Willem VanGemeren (Grand Rapids: Zondervan, 1997), 4:1093.

[55] He had to come up with such a system after sin had entered the world, not before. As if after the Fall, he said, 'Okay, since that happened, let's try this." I fully acknowledge God is outside of time, but he acts within time for our benefit and understanding.

[56] *Apollo 13*. Directed by Ron Howard. Written by Jim Lovell & Jeffrey Kluger and William Broyles, Jr. & Al Reinert. Performances by Tom Hanks, Gary Sinise, Ed Harris, Bill Paxton, and Kevin Bacon. Universal Pictures, 1995.

[57] John 5:19-20

[58] John 5:30-47

[59] Ephesians 2 teaches that because of the redemptive and salvific work of Jesus, non-Jews now had access to the God of Abraham. This access was granted by faith, contrasted with law-keeping of the Jews. Now, this faith, not birth, is the way into the family of God. The olive tree metaphor is employed to show the Gentile branch being grafted onto the Jewish tree via the mechanism of faith.

[60] It's more involved than just "believing" in a concept in your head. Repentance, mental assent, baptism, walking a new life, confessing the name of Jesus, et al. are all pieces of the "faith" pie, and all mentioned in the conversion accounts in the book of Acts.

[61] Hebrews 1:1-2. God no longer speaks in an audible voice because Jesus was the last, final, and ultimate revelation from God. If he spoke in some other way now, *that* wold be the last, final, and ultimate revelation from God, thereby diminishing the person and work of Jesus, who would then be the second-to-last revelation. And Jesus isn't second to anything.

[62] Most of this chapter comes courtesy of research on http://en.wikipedia.org/wiki/Bread, and from Peter Reinhart's TED Talk on Bread, found at http://www.ted.com/talks/peter_reinhart_on_bread.html

[63] Ibid. I concede this may be an etymological stretch, but the point is valid.

[64] Ibid.

[65] Ibid.

[66] 1 Sam. 15:22; Hosea 6:6; Amos 5:22-24; Psalm 50:7-23; Matt. 23:23

[67] I owe this insight to Dallas Willard's *The Divine Conspiracy*. Also found in Dallas Willard, "Spiritual Formation as a Natural Part of Salvation," Presented at the 2009 Wheaton Theology Conference (http://dwillard.org/articles/artview.asp?artID=135).

[68] I owe this insight to Derek Webb, Caedmon's Call, et al.

[69] Aside: My friend John D. Fortner in his lecture on the Holiness of God that if the Light on Day 1 Light and the Sun on Day 4 mixes you up and gives you problems, it's because you're trying to find science in this text. "Stop it," he used to say. "Find God in this text. Find peace and truth in this text. Find something to sink your teeth into and build your life around in this text. That's why it was written."

[70] John D. Fortner, *Holiness of God*, W.E.B West Lectures, Harding University Graduate School of Theology, 2005.

[71] Lev. 11: 44-45, et al.

[72] And let's not forget Commandments #1 and #2 ("No other gods before me," and "no idols"). Those first two commandments applied to oneself as much as to any golden shrine one might erect.

[73] I owe the genesis of this thought to Rob Bell's DVD, "Everything is Spiritual," (Grand Rapids: Zondervan) 2007.

[74] George MacDonald, *Annals of a Quiet Neighborhood*, chapter 28, 1892. Accessed via http://www.gutenberg.org/files/5773/5773-h/5773-h.htm This quote is often mis-cited as having come from C.S. Lewis.

[75] Let's not get hung up on whether Creation happened in 24-hour periods. That's totally not the point of the text. Let's move on.

[76] Rob Bell, Prophets/Poets/Preachers lecture (Grandville, Mich. : robbell.com), 2010.

[77] Rev. 21:21-22

[78] Cf. 1 Kings 8

[79] Luke 24:5

[80] Cf. 1 Cor. 13. I owe the genesis of this thought to Dr. Rodney Plunkett. Cf. 1 John 4:7-8

[81] This is a reimagining of Jesus' parable of the two builders, one of whom built his house on the sand and one of whom built his house on the rock. (Matt. 7:24-27)

[82] There's just such a pool on the rocks at Wemyss Bay in Scotland. I'm grateful to my friend Billy Wilson for giving me this insight into it and for telling this story much better than I ever could.